THE HEALING JOURNEY OF PET LOSS

A GUIDE TO HEALING YOUR HEARTBREAK & GRIEF FROM THE LOSS OF YOUR PET COMPANION

RUBY WOODS

ALECTRIC PUBLISHING

ABOUT THE AUTHOR

Ruby Woods has been a wife, mother, animal enthusiast, and dog trainer for over 25 years. She's spent her life working with all kinds of animals, but has a true love for harnessing a dog's obedience, agility, herding, and nose work. Ruby believes that when someone gets a canine friend, they know their beloved pet won't stay with them forever. And yet, we still choose to add the companion to the family, knowing the pain we are going to suffer at the end will still somehow be well worth it.

When it comes to the pet losses Ruby has experienced over her life, she loves the anonymous quote:

"It came to me that every time I lose a dog they take a piece of my heart with them, and every new dog that comes into my life gifts me with a piece of their heart. If I live long enough all the components of my heart will be dog & I will become as generous and loving as they are."

This book is in dedication to one of her shepherds who passed away, named Bullet, and all of the people that have experienced the painful loss of losing their pet companion and best friend.

CONTENTS

INTRODUCTION

The bond that you share with your pet is simple because the love you share is unconditional. You know exactly what I'm talking about. Your pet companion could tilt their head one way and blink with one eye, and you'd give them the world if you could. I've owned dogs my whole life, and I can tell you that it's not always rainbows and butterflies—especially during the training process. But they put up with the long hours of training without ever considering it hard work. They're just there for you, no matter what. While sweat drips down my face and the veins in my neck start bulging from shouting commands across the agility course, my beloved pet is just elated to be outside spending time with me.

Your pet doesn't care about the long list of mistakes you think you made today, yesterday, or any other day. They just want a warm place to sleep, a full bowl of food, and a couple of belly scratches here and there. This book recognizes the emotional connections well beyond just dogs or cats. When it comes to the diverse collection of creatures that are widely adored, you have to consider all the fur, feathers, fins, scales, or shells that have stolen the hearts of millions across the globe.

There are no words shared between you two, and yet, you have a lifetime of memories that transcends such trivial matters. You understand each other better than most people do. It seems like they'll always be there for you, but sadly, we know this is not possible. We'll explore some of the most valuable aspects of this bond. I'll show you how to keep your pet companion alive in spirit. There are so many ways to come to peace with this immense loss, even though it may not seem that way right now. I'll show you how to navigate through your period of grief so you can begin the healing process.

The memories you share with your pet companion are unparalleled. It's important that you try to focus on the joyful memories. Cherishing these memories with your pet companion is what keeps them alive in your heart. These memories will keep you upright as you tackle the tough parts like making the end-of-life decisions for your furry family member. There are several resources for pet owners during this time, but sometimes it's hard to seek them out without the proper guidance. That's what I'm here to help with. I want to facilitate a healthy healing process that is free of stress, anxiety, and guilt.

There is a whole lot of heartache that follows the loss of a pet companion. This is a fact that can't be ignored. Thankfully, with the strength of other people who have come together and shared their stories of grief and loss, we have figured out a better way to grieve the loss of a loved one without losing yourself in the process. Adjusting to life without them can be difficult, but it's essential to the healing process. We can't ignore the fact that the bond you share, or shared, with your pet transcends physical presences. The void left by their absence can be overwhelming. James Patterson gives us a unique way to view loss in his book, *Angel*.

"The weird, weird thing about devastating loss is that life actually goes on," says James Patterson in his book *Angel*. "When you're faced with a tragedy, a loss so huge that you have no idea how you can live through it, somehow, the world keeps turning, the seconds keep ticking."

When you find yourself in the depths of grief, it can feel as though the world around you fails to fully comprehend the immense magnitude of the pain you are experiencing. When that grief is directed towards the loss of a cherished pet, it can be even more challenging to find understanding and support. But acknowledging your grief, and understanding where it comes from, can give you a chance to step back and appreciate what your pet has given you. Those memories can't be taken from you. Sure, over time you start to think about them less, but those moments are forever cemented in the story of you. Your pet companion is a valuable aspect of your life, and that is worth the pain you'll experience at the end. These feelings are valid, and your emotions should be felt deeply. This is all a part of this difficult process we call healing.

With a little bit of time, compassion, and support, you'll find a way to step forward. We'll look at some ways you can honor the love and memory of your pet—who will reside within your heart forever. There hasn't been a moment in my life where I didn't have a pet companion by my side. With all of this love has also come immense loss. My beloved Shepherd, Bullet, is the inspiration behind this book. He left a lasting impact on me and my family. I'll use not just what I've learned through research, but what I've learned through experience to help you make it out of this dark spot in one piece. Patience is the most valuable asset in this process. Be patient with yourself, and always be kind. There is no *right* or *wrong* way to grieve.

We were put on this earth to experience things and learn from one another. I want to give you a space where you can learn all about pet loss without stretching yourself too thin. Be patient with yourself and read on. I can't promise it will be easy, but I can say that you'll be better prepared to handle those end-of-life decisions with a little help from someone who's been there.

1

LOVE BEYOND WORDS

"If you accept that pets can love us as much as we do them, then the logic is clear and cannot be denied. If you believe that there is a heaven for people, then they must be there, waiting for us, when we cross over," says Wallace Sife. *"Heaven is love, and pets always share that with us."*

THE DEEP BOND BETWEEN HUMANS AND PETS

I know I don't have to tell you how much love, joy, and affection that your pet companion brought to your life. You're probably no stranger to calling your pets cute nicknames like "sweetie," "handsome," or, the most recent fad, "fur baby." With this most recent development in the nickname game, we can actually see the way pets have begun to integrate into our families. It's hard to lose a family member, and you shouldn't try to diminish your grief after saying goodbye to your beloved fur baby.

The bond you share with your animal may even be so deeply intertwined with your well-being that it affects your health and your attitude day to day. According to the American Veterinary Medical Association (AVMA), a human-animal bond can be defined as "a mutually beneficial and dynamic relationship between people and animals." ("Human-animal bond" n.d.). Mutually beneficial is an understatement. This unique connection has many benefits, including stress reduction, mental support, improved mood, and it will definitely increase your levels of physical activity. That's why it's so difficult to let go when it's time (Deep Connections: The Power of the Human-Animal Bond" n.d.).

Now, we have proof that the loving relationship you share with your animal doesn't just affect your well-being, but that of your pet companion as well (Amiot, Bastian, and Martens 2016). Yes, that means every time your pet's dopey smile brought you out of a slump, their day brightened up a little bit too. Of course, animal friendships are very real and pose many benefits, but they shouldn't completely replace your human connections. You'll need a strong support system of non-animal beings after you've parted ways with your pet companion (Murray 2021).

For the most part, we can easily interpret a dog's signals and vice versa. We both have a need to be social, play, and create close bonds. We can also step in as social substitutes for the other's same-species family (Grandgeorge and Martine 2011). There are things we can't provide that their species will, but it's unique because it means that we truly are our pet's family, just as they are a part of ours.

When researchers examined the animal-human bond further, they found that modern-day pets actually activate a feedback loop of positive emotions between the human and their pet companion. This means oxytocin, dopamine, and other endorphins are shooting through your body just by looking at or thinking about each other. This has uncovered a whole new set of benefits for both parties including reduced stress and lower blood pressure (Amiot, Bastian, and Martens 2016). It can be hard to pinpoint the exact correlation between the animal-human bond and all of these subsequent benefits, because of all the outside factors that go into owning a pet. By this, I mean all the exercise, the grocery shopping, or even the pet play dates (Grandgeorge and Martine 2011). The positive effects of having a pet aren't always laid out perfectly in the proof, but it's pretty evident that there are several rewards and very little risk to adding a pet companion to the family.

Animals are especially rewarding when you consider the effects they can have on your children. Research has shown that owning a pet can not only improve family cohesion by giving everyone a similar task, but it can also increase your child's self-esteem. Kids can develop empathy in a clearer way when they are in charge of another living creature (Grandgeorge and Martine 2011). It also has the ability to reduce your child's anxiety through simple and unconditional love. Having a pet companion can act as a social substitute for classmates if they're lacking in the friendship area. Getting a chance to bond with other kids who have pets and share stories together helps improve your child's social skills, subsequently reducing any behavioral problems that were there beforehand (Amiot, Bastian, and Martens 2016). Also, exposure to animal fur or animal dander can actually help you build up immunity for certain allergies or asthma. Research has shown that kids who grow up in a pet-friendly household tend to report less trouble with allergies (Salo and Zeldin 2009).

New research has shown that when our canine friends look directly into our eyes, they activate the same hormonal response a baby would in our brains. This process is also called mutual gazing. What's even more interesting is that researchers also found that dogs experience a spike in their oxytocin levels when gazing at their human counterparts. This positive feedback loop is likely a factor in the domestication of canines (Grimm 2015).

According to the Human Animal Bond Research Institute, otherwise known as HABRI, this mutually beneficial relationship is "influenced by behaviors that are essential to the health and well-being of both." Our bond with our pet companion goes beyond the physical connections that we share. It's emotionally and psychologically rooted in us. These relationships are also what's called "situational," because not everyone gets those warm fuzzy feelings when they meet an animal. The relationship and the level of attachment are completely dependent on how you view the animal ("What is the Human-Animal

Bond?" n.d.). But why do we seek relationships with animals anyway?

As humans, we have an innate desire to seek out connections with living things—or even inanimate objects. Early humans likely jumped at the opportunity to become more connected with nature by initiating these animal encounters. While hunter and gatherer societies may have just scraped the surface by feeding them scraps and giving them bones, generations to follow would soon discover all of the similarities between humans and animals. Eventually, animals were celebrated by all societies in cultural ceremonies, worship, sacrifice, or just to use as symbolism. This eventually led to the anthropomorphization of these animals—or the ascribing of human characteristics to animals. Have you ever looked at your animal as it blinked one eye and cooed, "Look at that sweet face—they're winking at me"? This is anthropomorphization (Amiot, Bastian, and Martens 2016). The more we ascribe different human emotions to our pets' faces and behavior, the more they feel like just members of the family.

THE PHYSIOLOGICAL BENEFITS OF THE HUMAN-PET BOND

There are several perks to getting a pet companion that overpower the idea that it won't last forever. We've been using animals for companionship and assisted interventions for years, but only recently have we begun studying this mutually beneficial relationship. First, there is evidence that animals have been assisting the blind, soothing patients experiencing anxiety or depression, and providing companionship for the socially inept since the 19th century. Animal-assisted interventions (AAIs) are a valuable part of understanding the bond between humans and animals. (Amiot, Bastian, and Martens 2016). You'll also feel less lonely as your pet steps in for social support—ultimately boosting your mood overall (Hicklin and Piazza 2018).

When it comes to the physical side of owning a pet, a lot of the research varies by animal. If you want to understand the full extent of the physiological benefits you'll get from having a pet companion, you'll need to examine them by species.

"Is your goal to increase physical activity? Then you might benefit from owning a dog," says Dr. Layla Esposito, who oversees the News in Health Human-Animal Interaction Research Program (Hicklin and Piazza 2018). "You have to walk a dog several times a day and you're going to increase physical activity. If your goal is reducing stress, sometimes watching fish swim can result in a feeling of calmness. So, there's no one type that fits all."

Now several walks a day is a bit of an exaggeration. Sure, the more walks the better, but maybe you live in the city, or you don't have a neighborhood with a safe sidewalk to take. Maybe you have a pet turtle and walks just aren't *his thing*. There are plenty of other physical activities you can partake in with your pet to keep you both active. If you can get your pet's brain working, it's going to tire them out just as much as running them around your neighborhood. I like to work on specific training with my dogs. We work on agility courses, scent finds, and honing certain skills like darting through weave poles and hurdling over jumps. Again, don't make your turtle try this. Swimming in the kiddie pool will do for him.

You may be surprised to know that animals also tend to lower our triglyceride and cholesterol levels which are indicators of heart disease. It's been discovered that heart attack patients who are also pet owners live longer than non-pet owners. (Saunders et al. 2017). All of these combined benefits will increase your health because owning a pet teaches you about attention, intention, awareness, and compassion. When you pay more attention to your body and that of your pets, your awareness is increased and your actions have more intention behind them. The bond you have with your pet travels beyond logic. It practically has the power to heal you when you think about it (or at least keep you healthy). Owning a pet teaches you to be compassionate, not just to another being, but to yourself.

Recent research on the effects of owning an animal on your psychological well-being suggests that interacting with an animal can help you regulate your emotions more effectively. The interactions between you and your pet can provide a unique form of social support which can have a buffering effect against stressors. It hasn't been proven whether or not these buffering effects for stress are long-term, but this is mostly because research on this topic is so new. What we do know is that there's clear evidence of short-term differences in your physiological well-being that can be attributed to interacting with animals (Saunders et al. 2017).

THE PSYCHOLOGICAL BENEFITS OF OWNING A PET

Animal assistance in therapy, education, and even care for the elderly has increased in popularity over the past few years. The use of animal-assisted interventions (AAI) has been recommended for several kinds of patients including those who have autism, depression, anxiety, and any post-traumatic stress disorder. For those who have developmental disorders, this is extremely helpful in boosting sociability and improving confidence. Having a pet can leave you feeling happier overall (Beetz et al. 2012).

Spending some time with your Guinea pigs, cats, dogs, or whatever your companion may be, won't cure your depression per se. But having a pet around that you love and care for will give you a reason to smile when you get home. Spending time with them can lower your stress and allow you to feel a moments of peace as you forget about your stressors for the moment.

Another great benefit for your mental health is the addition of structure to your daily activities. Instead of racking your brain trying to figure out what to do with your day—wondering if you've done enough to be considered "productive"—you'll always have someone by your side waiting to do something with you. Even just providing daily care for your companion will give you a sense of purpose and achievement that is unparalleled. You may also feel more grounded and focused after accepting this responsibility. This is especially useful if you feel isolated or misunderstood by your peers. Maybe it's the fact that they can't stop or interrupt you, but pets are also *great* listeners ("Pets and Mental Health," n.d.). And not being able to respond with judgement (other than that ferocious side-eye) gives them a one up on any of your closest friends.

I know that you've probably already noticed the loss of all these wonderful benefits, but remembering how essential your pet was to your day-to-day life can bring you peace and validation for these intense emotions. People will say "It was just an animal," but you know that they were so much more. For some people, their fur baby is the only family they have around. For us, losing our beloved pet can feel like losing a piece of you.

PETS AS INTEGRAL FAMILY MEMBERS

Pets are so deeply intertwined with our lives that they've become an integral part of our families. For a long time, animals were only seen as a resource. Animals have been used as means of transportation, defense, and even food at times. (Sorry, don't let your pet chicken see this.) Now, instead of being a simple resource, pets are a source of joy and laughter in our households. So how did animals transition from being seen as mere means to an end to being regarded as actual members of the family?

With pet care on the rise, we see more and more pet owners pampering their little fur babies. Aside from pet care, we also have the grooming, the dressing, and the spoiling to consider. YouGov conducted a study with 1,275 adults—885 of which own a pet or a few pets—to see how many pet owners consider their pets part of the family. They looked at the percentage of people dressing their pets up, letting them sleep in their bed at night, and which owners are buying gifts for their pet companions. Two-thirds of the respondents said their pet sleeps with them, over half said they buy their companion gifts, and of course, almost 90% of respondents said that their pet was a valuable member of the family (Ballard 2019). You may have even referred to your pet companion as your best friend. Your pets don't judge, they just listen (and maybe give you a few side glances from time to time). That's another reason their presence is missed so dearly when they're gone. It seems like you'll never get that feeling back.

More and more couples without children are choosing to fill the space in their homes with a bouncing, beautiful fur baby instead. They're loyal and dependable, and it almost feels like they understand you better than most people do. Some people have decided to remain childless because pets imitate the same feelings of affection without all the added responsibilities of having a kid (Pascoe 2022). Let's face it, who doesn't love being able to snuggle up with your pet after a long day and just relax? And if you had a dog, you always knew to be prepared for a few slobbery kisses once your guard was down. It's these precious moments that truly make your pet a part of the family. Something unlocks inside of you when you see your pet all excited that you're home from work, and something breaks when you have to leave them behind for any reason.

Have you ever turned on some music or even the television for your pet before leaving the house? Do you have a separate stocking for your pal during Christmas time? Do you talk to them as if they can understand you? Oh, and I know you've seen all those adorable social media accounts people make for their pets. All of these are signs that your pet is not just a pet—they're family.

According to a survey done in Australia, many families have started to mimic this parent-child relationship with their pets. We're willing to go to extreme lengths to spoil our pets by investing in new surveillance technologies, buying them extra toys and other gifts, and some people even keep their dogs practically glued to their hips. Animal behavior experts have identified this behavior in dog and cat owners mostly, but there is plenty of evidence that people are speaking to their pets as though they can understand, and this number increases with each generation (Aubrey 2019).

More and more families are looking for ways to bring their pets just about anywhere. I used to bring Bullet with us on every family vacation. I just couldn't stomach the idea of leaving him under someone else's care. I can't even imagine making the choice to move somewhere that would have restricted Bullet's access to our home. I'd rather live in the same place for the rest of my life than give up Bullet for a few extra amenities. A lot of people feel the same way, so there has been an effort to increase awareness of pet-friendly housing and lodging ("Moving with a Pet..." n.d.). You wouldn't leave your kid home alone with an overfilled bowl of food and a couple of bowls of water, would you? That immense guilt that fills up inside of us pet owners when we're about to leave the house is just validation that we love these animals like they're our own children.

They'll be there when times get tough, and when the time comes, you'll be there to support them until the very end.

There's been an obvious shift in attitude regarding our fur babies (and the scaley ones too), so it's very evident why coping with pet loss has become increasingly harder over time (Aubrey 2019).

When our pets become our family, it's no wonder that the grief we feel when they pass is overwhelming. It may feel like a dark cloud has filled the house as everyone searches for a remnant of the past with their beloved pet. The heartbreak that washes over the whole house is surprising and suffocating. Despite knowing how much your pet means to you, it's hard to prepare for the moment they leave us. Instead of trying to anticipate the depth of emotions you feel, just let them flood through you. Let the pain flow through you, because then you have room to remember all of the cherished times from before. In the next chapter, I'll teach you how to do so without falling victim to any destructive habits. A lot of people let their grief get the better of them. Sometimes it's because they can't let go, but other times, it's because they just don't want to face these negative emotions. I'll show you how to face them without feeling like you're drowning.

ACTIVITY: LET'S TALK ABOUT THE BENEFITS

I want you to take a second to think about all of the wonderful benefits of bonding with your late pet. Take some time to jot down—or just imagine—a few of your favorite pastimes with your pet. Which of these benefits of the human-animal bond that we discussed resonated with you the most? Did your pet act like any ol' member of the family? What were their favorite snacks, toys, or areas of the house to lounge in? What were some of the ways you made them feel at home? Losing family is hard, but forgetting them is impossible—especially if you keep them alive in your heart. Take this time to remember all the incredible benefits of owning a pet and jot down some of the ones that changed your life for the better.

2

TREASURED MOMENTS

"We do not remember days, we remember moments," says Italian poet Cesare Pavese. *"The richness of life lies in memories we have forgotten."*

WELCOME TO THE FAMILY

Do you remember that wondrous moment you first brought your pet home? Maybe you can recall all the nervous energy and planning that took place those few weeks leading up to the big moment. There's a lot that goes into preparing for a new addition to the family. From setting up a space for them to gathering the appropriate supplies, everything is done carefully to ensure your new pet has a safe environment to live in. Whether you're setting up your fish tank with cool hideouts and trinkets, building a cat scratcher for a new feline friend, or collecting blankets and toys for your new puppy, the build-up is almost as exciting as actually meeting your newest family member.

Bullet was the very first male German Shepherd that I rescued. When the rescue service told me I could come in for an initial visit, I brought everything I would need to take him home with me that day. I loaded up a crate, a leash, and even a couple of dog toys. The drive to the shelter was a long one full of self-doubt and trepidation. As I got closer to the facility, I started to get nervous. At first, I was filled with doubts, but a part of me was still confident that this was the right decision. When I locked eyes with Bullet, all my worries and doubts washed away. His papers said he was about two years old, but his eyes still had that puppy sparkle. I had only seen photos of him leading up to this point, but when I was finally able to stroke his beautiful coat and stare into those dopey eyes, I fell in love. He had been in the pound for over two weeks, and the shelter employees said that his owners were not coming back.

I started to get nervous again. What if he was aggressive like the previous owners said? Maybe this was a mistake. But like I said, all of those worries fled my body the moment I met my sweet boy, Bullet. He was almost bashful in his introduction to me. It was like he could tell I wasn't just any other visitor. About fifteen minutes into our visit, I realized that I had forgotten the leash I'd brought in my car. I asked one of the rescue service workers to watch over Bullet while I grabbed the leash. The moment I left the room, I could hear him crying and whining so loudly that it echoed through the facility as I rushed to my car. It broke my heart that he thought I'd left so soon.

Obviously, I sprinted the rest of the way to my car, threw the door open, clumsily grabbed the leash, and charged full-speed back toward Bullet. When he saw my face again, he immediately stopped crying and started wagging his tail back and forth. It was like he could already smell that new home in the near future. As I loaded up Bullet into the crate and prepared to take him home, I was filled with an overwhelming amount of joy and appreciation. I wasn't thankful that his previous owners had abandoned him so carelessly, but I was thankful to have this opportunity to bring Bullet into my family. Bully breeds like shepherds, pit bulls, and bulldogs don't get a lot of attention at the shelters. In fact, the moment they're labeled as a bully breed or pit bull, these dogs have less of a chance of ever leaving the shelter (Levy, Olson, and Noby 2016). A dog's appearance can't really tell you anything about its behavior. That's why it was so important that I trusted my gut and made Bullet a permanent member of our family. He will be forever etched in the Woods family history books.

No amount of paperwork could have ever prepared me for how bright and keen his personality turned out to be. All my anxieties were immediately relieved the moment we got him home and into the backyard. If you've ever owned a dog before, then you probably know the term "zoomies." Bullet must have been named after his incredible ability to "zoom" because we couldn't get him to come back in for hours. He zoomed all around the yard like, well, a bullet, until he was panting and drool was dripping from his nose. I swear that smile didn't leave his face for a whole week. I'm so lucky to have had him in my life and to give him his.

THE PHASES OF A PET'S LIFE

We wish we could carry our pets with us through every moment in life. When you first meet your companion, you never consider what it's going to be like in a couple of years after they've gotten old and worn down by life. Everything is so new and exciting at first, so how could things ever get bad from here? As it turns out, it may be a little easier to cope with the passing of your beloved pet once you better understand their life cycle. Dogs, cats, and everything in between have a shorter lifespan than humans, but at least they'll be around longer than mosquitos in the summer or the in-laws visiting in the winter. Make those moments count by cherishing the time you do have with your beloved pet. Take an extra walk if you're feeling up to it. Go to the dog park from time to time if you're near one. Or, just don't forget to spoil your pets. I used to stuff Bullet's Christmas stocking with more treats and goodies than I would my in-laws (but let's keep that between us).

Each phase of a pet's life is memorable in its own way. Often-times, you'll see a complete personality change as your pet grows older. They might pick up some new habits along the way, or they may just decide they're not the same spry pup they used to be. Whatever the case may be, don't forget to be involved at every stage of their life, and use your limited time together to make new memories every day. Just because your pal can't run alongside you anymore doesn't mean they don't want to join the morning jog—maybe it's just time that you turn the jog into a walk so you can still spend time with your beloved companion.

A DOG'S LIFE

Just like when you have children, dogs go through different stages of development. At first, they'll need you for just about anything aside from making a mess and getting away with it—they just do that so well on their own. If you adopted your fur baby as a puppy, you probably got them anywhere from six to nine weeks after they were born. Puppies are very dependent on their mother before then—just flopping over one another clumsily until they reach her belly. All they can really do is crawl around ("Puppy Development…" n.d.). If you got your dog when they were a puppy, you probably remember a few clumsy moments. Maybe they enjoyed jumping on a toy that was bigger than their whole body, or their wobbly little head used to dip into the water bowl while they were drinking. Don't even get me started on puppy breath. There's nothing quite like it. At this adorable age, your pup could tear up a billion shoes and dig hundreds of holes in the backyard and still get away with it by batting their eyes and licking your nose. I wish I could have met Bullet during this stage of his life, but he was always a puppy in our eyes. He never stopped being curious about the world, even up until his last moments with us.

Socialization is another important aspect of puppyhood. Do you remember how your pup reacted when you first brought him home? You probably couldn't get them to stay in one spot the whole car ride as they soaked in all the new scenery. Maybe you let them stick their head out the window but instantly regretted it as your pup took the cue to try and shimmy out. Car rides, like everything else, will have a learning curve. After a few trials and errors, your dog will gain valuable insight into the proper behavior they should have at certain times. Try exposing your dog to doorbells, vacuums, crate training, car rides, and yes, obviously he should meet the mailman (this feud has to end somewhere). I once met a dog that hadn't been introduced to the hardwood floor until he was rescued by a loving family. When they got him home, he skied across the hardwood floor and instantly became overwhelmed. It took weeks to get him to step onto the hardwood without losing his balance. It's stuff like that which makes these moments unique to you and your furry companion.

Now, everyone who's ever owned a dog has some pretty hilarious training stories. Your pup is still trying to figure everything out, so they're bound to make some pretty funny mistakes. Bullet definitely wasn't a pro the first time he hit the agility course. In fact, it was a circus at times early on. After some repetition—and the realization that rewards were involved—we started to get in our groove. When it comes to training your pup, you probably started getting a little more intentional around ten weeks. You introduced them to the leash, rewarded them a lot with praise or treats, and in no time at all, your smart pup started picking up on cues around the house ("Puppy Development…" n.d.). I know with Bullet, every time I would pick the leash up, he was already sitting beside the door, head held high and tail sweeping the floor at maximum speed. His ears would perk up a little more when he heard us say "Ready?" or "You want to go?" And he was always down for a good car ride. Those good moments make me miss him dearly, but I'm glad they have permanent residency in my memories.

I can recall an especially funny car ride when Bullet and I were still learning the ins and outs of how each other acted in certain situations. About ten days into our journey together, I had him riding in the backseat of my crew-cab truck, with the back seats flipped down so he had all the room and a thick rug laid down for him. I stopped into a sandwich shop really quickly to grab some dinner. On my way home, I realized I should grab the mail from the post office as well. I parked and left the sandwiches sitting on the front seat, wrapped up neatly in their bag. I come back maybe two minutes later with no immediate concerns. Bullet was still in the back seat, though, he was licking his lips quite suspiciously. I looked over at the sandwiches and noticed there was a perfect snout-sized opening in one of the bags. I opened it up, and an entire half of a sandwich was missing. I always get a chuckle about how he grabbed himself a quick dinner, and almost got away with it, too. We both learned a valuable lesson that day. If you've ever had a pet that's snuck away with a piece of your food, you know exactly what I'm talking about. These mischievous moments turn into beautiful memories in time. These are the ones that will stick with you well after they're gone.

Bullet was such a happy dog from the moment we first got him home. Early on, I could see that he really appreciated his new life. He loved all of his toys, his dog beds, and the love he received on a daily basis. I never knew what the beginning of Bullet's life was like, but when you rescue a pet, you can feel the appreciation and joy radiate from them. You can feel the love in every joyful leap, tail wag, and slobbery kiss after a long day away from home. Try to remember all the times your pet made you laugh when they were learning not to jump on the table and beg for scraps. Try to remember that the joy that your pet brings you can be returned by a simple head scratch, treat, or words of praise, so don't hold back when it comes to showing your pet some love in return. There are still so many things for them to see in this world, and yet, hanging out within the four walls of your home is enough wonder and excitement for your little ball of joy. There are shadows to chase, mirrors to bark at, and plenty of stinky socks to destroy. What more could a pup need?

The thing that has the biggest impact on your pup's personality is *you*. Take the puppy stage one step at a time. For pet parents, these moments are just as precious and rewarding as spending time with a newborn baby. They won't be this small for very long at all. In fact, puppyhood will practically fly by. You may not even remember how small they were until you find old pictures of them. All dogs are different, just like people are. Don't expect your pup to adjust as quickly as the ones who came before. There is a certain level of trust that goes into training a dog to do what you say. I never expected Bullet to catch onto agility training as quickly as some of the others who came before him. But he surprised us all when he hit the course ready to rock and roll. Even though he'd never been exposed to so many obstacles and the smell of other dogs, he waited patiently for commands (or, more likely, treats). I remember the first time he took off over a jump. He practically broke it in half belly flopping on top of it. And yet, he still jogged back over to me with an unbelievably dopey smile on his face.

Bullet was a brave soul, and I could tell he trusted me from the beginning. His personality was so outgoing. This helped his transition immensely. Living in Alaska, my father had a small float plane—a Maule M7–which would seat four people. He had built an amazing cabin up north, close to Petersville, Alaska. It was pretty remote, so most of the time, we'd have to fly in. This was about a 35-minute flight. Fishing season was such a great time to travel up there with the family, and since Bullet was now a part of the family, he was going to have to learn to fly. On his first trip in the plane, he was visibly concerned. He shook a little once the engine fired up, as it was quite loud in the cockpit. We sat in the backseat, and as the plane started up, he put both his front feet—and most of his weight—onto my thighs. I gently held my hands over his ears and tried to calm him down. Bullet had no idea what was about to come next. One moment, we were skidding across the water, and the next, we were looking down on the lake and off into the sunset. He stayed pretty calm the entire flight, but once we landed, he was elated to jump onto the dock and be on solid ground. After that, he became a regular airman. He was taking at least a dozen flights a year—sometimes falling asleep in my lap, and other times just gazing down out of the window. Times like this make me feel happy about what a great life we gave him.

Bullet really grew into a confident, kind, and sweet young man. I wasn't looking for a puppy when I found him, and I was just happy to be able to make the rest of his time with us memorable. The life expectancy of a dog can depend on their breed, their size, and of course, pre-existing medical conditions. To ensure Bullet's golden years were filled with nothing but love and happiness, I made sure to take him to the vet for regular checkups. As dogs age, their joints will stiffen and they'll be far less energetic. This is about the time when you should slow things down and start making some changes to help your pal feel comfortable. Your vet may suggest certain medications or lifestyle changes (like no more scraps from the dinner table!) ("Puppy to Senior…" 2022). But the most important part about seniority is taking the time to reminisce on your life together with your best friend.

Bullet changed the way he ate as he got older, and it used to make us laugh so hard. Instead of standing up over his bowl, one day, he just started lying down in front of it. I got him a small shelf to put the bowl on so that he wouldn't strain his neck so much, but he wasn't worried about all that. All he wanted was some comfort. What was even funnier was the way he'd pick up one piece of dog food at a time and drop it on the floor. From its place on the floor, Bullet would slurp the singular piece of dog food up, chew it until it was gone, and then start the process all over. Sure, it took longer, but he seemed to enjoy it, and the whole house got a good laugh out of it. Bring up weird behavior changes with your vet, but try not to worry too much. Instead, soak in these odd moments to cherish well after they're gone. After all, senior dogs are just puppies trapped in an aging body. They can still have fun, too.

CATS, HAMSTERS, AND EVERYTHING IN BETWEEN

If you've owned a cat, you know their love isn't as easily won by a few squeaky toys and treats. Yet, our bond with these mischievous little bundles of joy is equally as strong as the one we share with our canine friends. Sure, they need their vaccinations, checkups, and everything else any other pet needs, but don't expect them to snuggle up with you the moment your butt hits the couch, or go bananas when you get home from work. They, too, are playful and full of endless curiosity, but trust works a little differently with cats.

When your cat finally accepts you as their human family, it's beyond rewarding. If you adopted, then your cat may have been all hisses and scratches at first until they realized you're the new guy in charge of food. Like dogs, cats are more impressionable at a young age, so they'll be developing mentally and emotionally for about the first two years. At this stage, your kitten was probably more like a fur bullet bolting around the house from corner to corner. Their curiosity knows no bounds. They'll climb on the fridge, they'll get behind the washer, and they'll definitely try to break into the cabinet where you keep the treats. Their care needs evolve over time, but with proper nutrition, plenty of water, and some exercise, your furry friend could stick around for over fifteen years (Syufy 2019).

It can take up to a year and a half for your cat's personality to start shining through, but observing their body language is a great way to get some insight into who they are. Take a mental note of the way your cat leaps six feet into the air when a semi-truck passes by the house. How did your furry friend react when they met a dog for the first time? You probably noticed that your cat became less timid and more confident after kittenhood, but as they got to be up in the senior age range, their behavior likely switched again (W., Emily n.d.). I'm sure you can recall a few habits your cat picked up and then grew tired of over the years. Remember how they used to chase your shoestrings around as a kitten? Or the way they'd go ballistic over that little laser on the floor? Memories like this can be painful to draw upon, but they allow us to keep our fur babies alive in our hearts forever.

Hamsters and guinea pigs are small, but they have big hearts. When handled properly they're not skittish, and they make great pets for children. They have such a wide range of person-alities, and they are social creatures (so it's best to buy in pairs). Hamsters can live up to three years, and guinea pigs a bit longer at nearly seven years (Trautner 2017). Nobody is going to judge you for talking to your pet companions, no matter how small they may be.

Birds practically live forever. You probably grew up *with* your feathery friend—learning the ropes of life together. They're pretty easy to care for, and some species can live more than 100 years. Owning a bird is a lot like having a forever-toddler. Maybe you owned one that has the ability to mimic you. You probably have a ton of great memories trying to get them to say things that will make you laugh. Turtles, too, live an exception-ally long life. You probably spent many summers soaking up the sun together or taking a dip in the pool (though I'm sure you were told not to take your scaley friend to any public pools). There are a lot of reptiles that make excellent, long-term companions. Lizards, snakes, and other reptiles are also fascinating creatures.

Though I've never owned one myself, I can imagine losing your pocket-size pet companion is just as sad as losing a friend. Some of them can even be affectionate once they get used to you (Trautner 2017). Can you recall a fun memory with your reptile companion that made you smile ear to ear? Maybe your lizard liked to mount your shoulder and snuggle your neck or get tangled in your hair. Don't get too caught up in missing them when you're recalling these memories, either. Try to let yourself laugh every now and again. I'm sure it was pretty funny watching your pet hamster realize just how fast *"too fast"* is on his wheel, or hearing your bird repeat a curse word you slipped up and said earlier.

THROUGH YOUR PET'S EYES

Let's take a moment to step into your pet's perspective:

Hi, I'm your newest addition to the family, and my world has just opened up for the first time. No longer am I trapped in a dark, gloomy cage waiting for my forever home. I finally found it. Even the car ride to the house is filled with new stuff. There are so many new smells, new people to sniff, and new sights to see. My world finally has color. Maybe not *all* the colors, but I definitely haven't seen a sky so bright since I was a pup.

The second we stepped through those doors, my life began. I was bombarded with new toys, a new place to lay my head at night, and food out the wazoo. These wonderful, gigantic beings keep talking to me in a different language. I don't under-stand a single word of it, but they like it when I try to respond anyway. The giants are always picking me up and moving me around to snuggle. I'd get dizzy if I didn't love it so much. I've never been so happy in my life.

I've picked up on a few things over the past few years. Some-times the giants get sad and they like to try and talk to me even more. They'll go on and on, and they won't even wait for me to respond. I hate it when it starts raining from their eyes. I try to do all the stuff that they laugh at in order to make them smile. This usually works in no time. If it doesn't, we usually just hang out in bed or on the couch for a really long time. I really love hanging out on the giant's bed. It's way more comfortable than mine.

Sometimes, my new family gives me what they call "treats," and it fires up all my senses. When I'm not feeling good, I get even more attention. As I get older, sometimes I get scared that I won't be able to cheer my giant up anymore. It gets harder for me to keep my energy up as I get older, but I'd do anything to make sure they'll be happy, even when I'm gone. We've made so many memories together that will last forever. I only hope that my giant holds them just as near and dear as I do.

ACTIVITY: REFLECT ON JOYFUL MEMORIES WITH YOUR BELOVED PET

Now, we've talked a lot about the wondrous perks of being a pet parent, but what were your favorite parts? Did you enjoy the high-energy training sessions, or were you more of a lay-on-the-couch-with-them-all-day kind of parent? To reinforce those happy memories with your pet, take this time to jot down some of your favorite moments together. Try to reflect on specific moments with your pet that brought a smile to your face. Vividly describe your feelings in those moments, and reflect on why these memories hold a special place in your heart. Maybe you have a favorite adventure or outing with your pet. What made those trips so special? Have you experienced a challenging or difficult period in your life where your pet companion was there to guide you through? How did their presence and unconditional love bring you out of your slump? And don't forget to sprinkle in those funny and playful memories that made you forget about the stress of life for just a moment.

3

GUIDED BY LOVE

"Then one day we suddenly realized that we had been keeping him alive not because it was good for him, but because it was good for us, because it was too hard to make the decision to let him go," says Anna Quindlen in her book *Good Dog. Stay.*

KNOWING YOUR PET'S NEEDS AND PREFERENCES

I know that making the right decisions for your pet near the end of their life can be hard. You should find peace in knowing that you did the best thing for your beloved pet because you were the only one who really understood them. Understanding your dog's physical, emotional, and social needs is important because it gives you the opportunity to provide the best possible care. We want to keep your pets happy and healthy for as long as possible. Familiarizing yourself with their typical behaviors, routines, and habits establishes a baseline for what's "normal," and gives you a chance to recognize when something is out of the norm. You can't extend their life forever, but the better care you take of your pet, the longer they tend to stick around.

There are a few common warning signs you should look out for when trying to gauge whether or not your pet needs to take a trip to the vet. Changes in eating or drinking habits, shortness of breath, vomiting, shakiness, and loss of balance are all signs that something serious could be wrong with your pet. You may want to take them to the vet and get these symptoms checked out ("10 Warning Signs Your Dog…" n.d.).

Most important of all, you should trust your gut. If you think something is wrong with your beloved pet, then you should take the appropriate measures to ensure they're in good health. You, as the primary caregiver for your pet, have a unique insight into your pet's behavior and their needs. There have been several cases where simply paying attention has given a pet a second chance at life. A lot of pet parent's get crap for being "overprotective," but we're almost always right when we get that *feeling* that something is wrong with our furry friends. Some of us may be a little protective, but it's because we want what is best for our pets, especially when they're hurting. When our fur babies are in pain, so are we.

Lots of vets try their hardest to catch everything they possibly can in their screenings and tests, but sometimes, things fall through the cracks. As a pet owner, if you know something is wrong, it's always best to be persistent. A veterinarian shared a story online of an older dog and an overprotective owner. According to the owner, the elderly dog was eating slower, not following her owner around the house, and generally wasn't as energetic. The vet did all of the necessary screenings, but nothing showed up. After a while, they summed it up to aging and tried to dismiss the idea of underlying illness. The owner insisted they run the tests again, and this time, the vet found several tumors in the dog's lungs. He'd had cancer the whole time, and it would have gone undetected had the owner not spoken out and continued to push for proper care (Corgimatic 2016).

Your role as their caregiver is invaluable. You're the one who knows their behavior and their preferences the best. If you want proof of a strong bond, then take a look at some more outstanding examples of pet parents who *knew* something was wrong with their pet despite everyone else's doubts. A woman walked into the vet with her dog after it didn't eat dinner for one night. She was convinced that her dog had gastric dilatation-volvulus (or GDV). This is a life-threatening disorder—most often seen in large breeds—where the stomach fills with gas, causing them to bloat. Sometimes, the disease won't progress past this bloat, but other times, the gas-filled stomach can twist itself up, blocking the entrance and exit of the stomach. The vet tried to tell her that there would be clear signs of GDV before she'd even have to consider taking her dog to the vet, but she insisted they run the tests anyway. Turns out, she was absolutely right (Sabeljax 2016). Sometimes, being the "crazy" pet owner isn't so crazy after all.

END-OF-LIFE CARE AND DECISION MAKING

Your insight is especially important when it comes to the final stages of your pet's life cycle. It can feel overwhelming at times, but again, remember all of the incredible memories that you made together when they were happy and healthy. Now, it's time to help them find peace. None of us want to see our companions in pain. Knowing when to say goodbye to your pet is one of the hardest things to figure out. But we're lucky to have the time that we do with our beloved pets. Take this opportunity to reflect on the fact that you had the chance to give them a good life, and they were a valuable piece of yours.

So many questions run through your head when you start to realize your pet is getting older. Should you take certain measures to prolong their life, or are they in too much pain? Is there a way to objectively measure their quality of life just by their behavior alone? How can you make your pet comfortable as they near the end of their life? Sometimes, the signs are pretty clear. Maybe your pet has begun to show signs of pain, such as having trouble getting up and down from the couch or navigating the stairs. Or, maybe your pet has stopped eating or drinking at a normal rate. If it seems like your pet is more lethargic and not as excited to partake in their previously-loved activities, then maybe they're telling you that it's time to slow things down.

Before you can think about making things comfortable for your pet at the end of their life, you should understand what's making them uncomfortable. As animals age, they're more susceptible to disease and infection. Some people aren't in the right place financially to take extreme measures to keep their pet along for the long ride. Surgeries, prescriptions, and other veterinarian care can be pretty expensive. When you are met with a choice of letting go or holding on, make sure you're looking at all of the options—and the ones that are best for you ("How to Know Whether Your Pet..." n.d.). Everyone wants to believe that money is no object when it comes to providing for our family, but this just isn't reality. Don't let other people guilt you into making decisions that aren't the best for you or your beloved companion. Remember, you two understand each other in a way no one else does. We hold the keys to our pet's life close to our hearts, and even when it's hard to let go, we have to do what's best for our furry friends.

A veterinary oncologist, Dr. Alice Villlobos, has developed a scale that can help dog owners measure their beloved pet's quality of life. It provides information for both pet parents and vets alike, so together you can make the best plan possible for your furry friend. By using a scale that looks at seven different categories, you can average your pet's quality of life based on their levels of hurt, hunger, hydration, hygiene, happiness, mobility, and whether or not they have more good days than bad (Hunter n.d.). Once you have a pretty good idea of how your pet is dealing with each of these categories, you can better understand how much pain your pet may be going through, and make an informed decision.

If you have a primary care vet, then they should be intimately involved with the geriatric care of your fur baby. They can help paint that bigger picture for you when things seem too over-whelming to grasp. They'll also try to provide you with as many options as possible. Vets can help you set up a geriatric care plan and help you decide when it's truly the right moment to let go ("How to Know Whether Your Pet…" n.d.). This takes out a lot of the guilt and self-doubt when it comes to making end-of-life decisions for your best pal.

HOW TO EMOTIONALLY PREPARE YOURSELF

There isn't a singular way to prepare for the death of your companion. I don't have a magic spell that can make you oblivious to the pain that is yet to come, or a bandaid that patches up your heart when they're gone. I can, however, give you a few tips to emotionally prepare yourself for these moments. I wish I had taken more time to prepare for the loss of Bullet. We had a dog many years ago, and my sweet Bullet always reminded me of him. Our old dog gave us several signs that it was his time to go, and while we weren't ready, we chose to soak in those last few weeks. We weren't busy holding on to the past. Instead, we tried to make as many new memories as we could, and laughed about all the great stories we already had to tell. Having that time to soak up was a blessing in itself though. We weren't so lucky with Bullet. The best thing you can do for your pet when they're getting close to the end is to remain in the present. Do things that bring you both joy and do them often (Monahan 2022). You may have to hold your pal up these days so they can look out the window, but there's no reason to be sad about that. It just gives you another reason to be close to your pet.

Sure, your dog might not be as excited to get to the park as they were when they were a pup, but if you pay close attention, you'll see your little bundle of joy soaking in all the precious moments life has to offer. You don't have to take strenuous hikes with your aging buddy to fill your last few months together. Instead, you could make a ramp for the stairs in the backyard so it's easier for your companion to walk outside whenever they want. Or maybe, your cat has a hard time leaping up on the counter to drink out of the faucet these days. You can make a ramp with carpet on it so he can get up with ease, or you can find a pet water fountain at your nearest pet shop. It's all about spending time together and making sure your pet is as comfortable as they can be (Monahan 2022).

Coming to terms with the end of your pet's life should be done sooner rather than later because having plenty of time to prepare is essential to your emotional well-being. People who have had their pet's life cut short tragically have said that making the decision to put them down was a lot harder without the proper time to prepare (Monahan 2022). Instead of trying to ignore the signs, embrace your pet and remind them every day how much you love them until the end.

According to bioethicist and writer, Jessica Pierce, Ph.D., preparing for the death of your pet serves three purposes. By preparing sooner rather than later, you're inviting everyone to grasp the reality that death is inevitable. I know that it sounds bleak, but trying to ignore it for too long will put you in this strange space of denial (Pierce 2021). Denial can be more painful than just accepting the sad truth that our beloved pets can't stick around forever. It can lead to a much bleaker reality where you're unable to accept your own feelings, and you constantly suppress your true emotions (Hodge 2023). If you start preparing sooner rather than later, you have plenty of time to figure out the practical stuff early on so that those last few days are spent worry-free with your pet by your side. Lastly, preparing for the death of your pet gives you time to explore the many options available to you. Maybe you don't want your beloved pet to pass in a clinical setting. Maybe you'd feel more comfortable finding a veterinarian who can come to your home for the euthanasia process (Pierce 2021). Whatever your decision may be, being prepared takes a lot of the pressure off you and your family.

THINGS YOU SHOULD CONSIDER

I know you probably don't want to hear this, but there are several practical planning elements that need to be taken care of on top of preparing yourself emotionally. There's plenty of medical stuff to consider, like your budget for treatment plans, post-mortem body storage and transport, and what you plan to do with their body. Are you planning to cremate or bury them? Will you be present? Some people have chosen to bury their pets in a human cemetery that allows owners to purchase adjoining plots (Pierce 2021). Maybe you have a place on your own property where you'd like to bury. Whatever your choices may be, you should try to set these plans into motion quickly so you can spend the rest of your time cherishing each moment and making life-long memories with your pet companion.

If you have kids or other close family members, you may also need to consider how you're going to incorporate them into the decision-making process. Laurel Lagoni, President of World by the Tail, Inc. and director of the Veterinary Wisdom Resource Center, released a report in 2011 on the nine questions you should consider while planning your pet's end-of-life care. We've already covered most of them, such as looking over different treatment options and comparing them to your budget, but she also thinks it's important to consider how you'll involve your children in the decision-making process. She urges you to educate your children about the process by accessing certain resources available to you. Maybe consider bringing your kids along to a few vet visits so they can hear how this whole geriatric-pet-care thing works. They might even better understand the passing of their beloved pet after listening to it from a professional's point of view (Lagoni 2014).

Question five was my favorite. "What do you think your pet wants?" Lagoni asks. She asks you to consider what signs your pet has already given you that they're no longer enjoying life. Is your pet still enjoying time outside? What about their food? Do they like anything about their daily routine anymore? Considering the amount that your pet is suffering is a very essential part of coming to terms with the decision to let go. As Lagoni says, "Pain can be medicated, but suffering is harder to define and treat." (Lagoni 2014). Perhaps you've started to notice your dog limping around the house, or whimpering as they get up on the couch. You could put a splint on your dog and hope that it helps them get around better, but if their mobility continues to decrease, then they're probably suffering from a much deeper condition.

Make sure that you're asking all of the appropriate questions during the last few visits to the vet. Inquire about the how, when, and where of the euthanasia process. If you're uncomfortable with the steps your pet's primary care provider takes, then consider other end-of-life options for your pet. There are plenty of private services that deal with these sorts of things. You want to make sure that you can say goodbye properly. You won't be stuck wondering if you did what was best for you and your pal after they're gone if you take the appropriate time to ask questions and research the right options for you (Lagoni 2014). Some people have regretted not doing the at-home euthanasia process after hearing how much peace it has brought other families. Others have said they wished they would have cremated their pet instead of burying them—cementing them in one place forever. Most of these people weren't even aware that there were other options out there for them and their beloved pets aside from going to a vet. Personally, I think that if your pet has given you plenty of signs that it's their time to go, you should lay a blanket out on the lawn and lay there with them as they pass. It takes the stress off of all the parties involved, and you get to lay there petting your best pal one last time under the sun.

Lagoni goes on to ask what you'd like to say to your pet before they die, as taking a meaningful action can help you feel more prepared emotionally to let them go (Lagoni 2014). Maybe you could do a last hike up your favorite trail, or visit your dog's favorite hot dog stand. Take a moment to appreciate all the love and joy your pet has brought you. I like to think that Bullet was glad to spend his last good days up in Oregon on our annual family vacation. He loved the plane rides, the long walks, and the beautiful scenery just as much as we did. He waited to take a turn for the worst until after that one, final trip so that we could make those final moments last.

MAKING THEM FEEL LOVED

The last days with your pet are undoubtedly the hardest. While it may be difficult to see the light during these dark days, there are several ways to soften the blow of losing your four-legged family member. Some ways to bring a little more joy back to the family include finishing a bucket list of things you'd like to do with your pet, inviting some extended family over to come say their goodbyes (and get their snuggles in), pampering your pet with special treats, and taking some extra photos and videos to remember all of the good times you had together. You may consider making some sort of memento, like a paw print in clay or a mound of their snout (Anderson 2022). Get your cuddles and chitchats in now, because it may be the last time you guys get to have these momentous one-sided conversations. Whatever you decide to do, just make the most of it. Hold them close, like you'll never let go. Tell them you love them, and thank them for always being there for you no matter what.

Making your pet feel comfortable during their last days is all you really can do. Don't rack your brain trying to figure out if you could have done something more in their lifetime to avoid this horrible moment. Hell, we all could have done something different for our companions, but it wouldn't have changed a thing. Don't kick yourself for not having a portrait done of you two to hang over the fireplace, or for not keeping the leash you had when they were just a pup. You loved them deeply, and your bond isn't diminished just because you don't have enough pictures to make a photo collage for a memorial ceremony. Maybe you set up a bed that made it easier for your pal to get up and lay down without too much effort. Or, maybe you put a blanket over them during the winter months to help ease the arthritis pain (Anderson 2022). Your pal was thankful, and you can take pride in the fact that you made those last few weeks more comfortable for them. It's only natural that you feel those tiny pings of guilt in your chest, but I'm here to tell you that it's just your heart breaking. A broken heart can be mended, but you'll drown in that guilt. Make these last moments about you and your pet only, because these are the moments you'll remember forever.

Mindy Waite, Ph.D., and Julie Burgess—two renowned dog behaviourists and trainers—made a bucket list of 18 different things that you should consider doing before putting your dog to sleep. When we had to make the decision to put Bullet to rest, I scoured the training books on my shelf and every corner of the internet, looking for ways to make this time easier. I wanted to find things that would make him happy, but deep down, I knew that I was doing it for me, too. Bullet wanted to keep his energy up just to put a smile on my face, so I wanted these last moments to be special for us both. What was unique about Waite and Burgess's article was that they said it was okay to have "multiple final days" with your pet if they're up for it. You don't want to miss out on your final adventure with your pal, but maybe after that, they're still feeling energetic. If your pet lives longer than you expected, take those precious moments and spend them doing more adventures. Maybe take a nice drive to a secluded park, or visit the beach in the off-season. You don't want to overwhelm them, but it is nice to get out and spend some quality time together, especially if it gives you a chance to capture some more photos of your beloved pet (Burgess and Waite 2023).

Remember when I said that you know your pet's preferences better than anyone else? Turns out, identifying these preferences and making them a reality can also bring some joy back to both of your lives during the last few days. It's a small gesture, but if you know your pal loves a good turkey sub (and the doctor said it was okay) then go ahead and spoil them. Or, maybe your dog just loves a good car ride where they can soak up all the sun and smells. Making your pet feel happy and content is essential to making their last few days comfortable (Burgess and Waite 2023).

Bullet had more spunk toward the end than we could have imagined. One day we're having a good time in Oregon soaking in the sun, the next, we're rushing to the emergency veterinary clinic because he'd finally stopped eating. If I had known that these were my final moments with him, I would have tried to be more present. I would have taken more pictures, given him a few extra treats, and I would have reminded him how much he meant to me. At least we were able to maintain a fairly "normal" schedule for him. Maybe that made him feel less scared. Waite and Burgess recommend keeping your regular routine to lower your pet's stress levels as they near the end. I know that these days feel anything *but* normal, but it's important to try your best for the sake of your pet's health (Burgess and Waite 2023). Toss a ball around in the backyard, eat meals at regular times, and try to keep your spirits up. It's hard watching your pet experience cognitive difficulties or start to get weaker, but with the help of your vet, you can better understand your pet's pain and help make them more comfortable.

Euthanizing your pet is such a complicated way to lose a pet. Some people worry their pal may have had a few good years left in them, and others worry that they waited too long to give their furry friend some peace. But that's why it's so important that you talk to your vet throughout this whole process. Most vets will be hesitant to euthanize unless there truly is no hope for recovery. Always keep in mind that you did everything in your power to care for your pet. There is no one on this earth better suited to make end-of-life decisions for your pet. And remember, you're doing this *for* them, not *to* them. You gave them a great life, and you should cherish those memories instead of wallowing in your self-doubt and grief.

YOU'RE NOT ALONE

Nobody can put a timeline on grief. Let it flow through you, and don't try to apologize or diminish it. We all know the stages of grief—denial, anger, bargaining, sadness, and acceptance— but it's important you allow yourself to work through each of these stages. Instead of feeling angry at the world for taking your best friend, be grateful for the life you shared (Burnett- Brown 2022). I still like to imagine Bullet wagging his tail furi- ously as he tries to wedge his way between my legs as I come in through the front door. I can hear his little grunts and pants in my head as I make my way to the kitchen with a bag of fresh sandwiches from that local sandwich shop. These things never leave you, so don't worry; your pet is never *really* gone for good.

Remember when I said that you'll need a support system during this time? Your pet has provided their unwavering support and love for all these years, and now it's time for you to lean on the other people who love you dearly. A support system can offer their condolences and provide help in areas you may not have realized beforehand. Your support system can be family, friends, or even coworkers who know the kind of joy that your pal brought to your life (Burgess and Waite 2023). Consider reaching out to people who can relate to your experiences. This can be within your support group, or on different support group sites and social media. Your neighbors might even be an untapped resource for emotional support. There are plenty of different ways that people have had to say farewell to their beloved pets. Even when you know you're just doing your best, it's still comforting to know that you're not alone.

If you have ever chosen to go through an at-home euthanasia process, or if you're considering this option for your beloved pet, you may find comfort in knowing that there are others who found this to be a very comforting and non-clinical way to lay their pet to rest. On an online forum, someone shared a story about the steak dinner they cooked the night the vet came to their home to administer the shot. All of their pet's favorite people were invited over, and he got his very own plate of cut-up steak. They held him as the shot was administered, and he "passed away peacefully, with all his best friends and family around" (Asrtaldays83 2022).

On the same thread, someone else shared their experience with saying their last goodbyes from home. As their pup lay down beside him on the floor, he told him what a good boy he was over and over again. After he passed, the vets took care of everything, including the cremation. The man was able to go walk his beloved pet's favorite trail while the vets took care of it all. By the time the man had returned from his hike with dried tears stuck to his cheeks, the ashes were delivered to him, and then they were gone. Things were smooth, and he didn't have to stress about a thing along the way. He wishes he'd known about these kinds of options for his other fur baby who had to be put down many years ago (Asrtaldays83 2022).

One man chose to do at-home euthanasia because his dog hated the vet. His poor pup would whimper and cry every time he had to go, so he knew that they had to find another option. He recalls that it was a "very peaceful" experience, and he couldn't have picked a better way to say goodbye to his best friend. Being surrounded by "all of his favorite people," and allowing him to eat "some of the forbidden foods he always wanted to try" made it easier to let go (RackaGack 2022). Your pet's last days are just as worthy of being memorable as the first ones. I know it hurts, but all you can do in those final moments is hold your pet close and tell them one last time how much you love them. At-home euthanasia makes those last moments a little more bearable.

Some people have multiple dogs at home who might be hurt and confused if their owners left with one of their friends and didn't come home with them. Pet parents with two or more fur babies wonder if their other pets will be depressed after the loss of their companion. It's a fair thought. I mean, after all, you miss them dearly and you can't even speak the same language. A woman shared her experience with at-home euthanasia from the perspective of someone with multiple dogs. She said that the process really helped her beagle understand that her companion was now gone. "They need to understand what's happening," she wrote on the online forum (MrsNuggs 2022).

Louie the puggle and Jake the Labrador were best friends. They often slept side by side, and even after Jake passed away on the living room floor, Louie wouldn't leave his side. Louie knew his friend was getting sick probably before their owners did. That didn't make it any easier for poor Louie. He needed extra comforting and coaxing to finally leave his best friend, Jake, so that his body could be buried in the yard ("Is It Beneficial to Have Other Pets Present..." 2015). Of course, you shouldn't force your companion pets to be present if they don't want to be, but if they're as close as Jake and Louie were, then maybe consider at least keeping them in the same room while their friend is put to rest.

You don't always have the time to plan something as poetic as a peaceful death at home. Many people have come forward to share their experience of losing their pet at the veterinarian hospital to show others that they're not alone in their pain. It can be a very hard place to say goodbye to your best friend, and it takes a good bit of mental strength.

One man on an online forum said that he didn't want his poor cat to see his "ugly crying in its face" so he decided to perk up a bit and sing his cat some of their favorite songs he used to sing.

Another woman said that she regrets having a panic attack as her cat of twenty years passed in the vet's office. She didn't try to pull it together. Instead, she cried into her cat's belly until there was no more soft rising and falling (Foospork 2023). I don't think she, or anyone else, should feel regret for letting those emotions boil over. In fact, if you didn't ugly cry over the loss of your best friend, then maybe *that* is weird. But getting upset, especially at the vet's office, is perfectly normal. It might be impossible not to fall apart during those last few moments. Don't feel bad for shedding a tear or two. A lot of people seem to believe that keeping a happy face for your pet will make it easier for them as they go, but what about how you feel? I'm not saying you should shake your fist at the sky and curse the world for taking your pet too soon, but it's okay to let that pain show. It kind of feels like an out-of-body experience, doesn't it? Time moves slowly and indescribably fast simultaneously. You might even lose the ability to say anything at all. One woman talks about how the suffering in that moment caused her to lose time (Beautiful-Page3135 2023): "Within 10 minutes of us walking in the door, he was at peace," she wrote. "It didn't feel like 10 minutes...it simultaneously felt like an eternity and the blink of an eye. As much as it hurt—hell it's the only time in my life I've really cried over a loss—it was the kind thing to do."

I know someone who, just like me, lost their beloved pet so quickly, that they barely got a chance to say goodbye. Ace was a beautiful German Shepard with so much energy, even to his last day. His hips had started to bother him more and more, and the vet warned everyone that his time was starting to creep up on him. In the middle of the night, he started bleeding uncontrollably out of his nose. He was rushed to an emergency clinic, where the vets said they couldn't find anything wrong with him. They slowed the bleeding and sent him home to let in other patients, and by the time he got home, he'd passed away in the car. His family piled in the car beside him and held him until they got back to the very same vet as before. It was hard having to make all the decisions right then and there about what to do with the body, but the emergency veterinary clinic provided all the necessary help, and his family was sent home with a clay paw print and a box of Ace's ashes.

There is no "right way" to say goodbye to your beloved pet. You don't always have the time, money, or emotional capacity to do what others might think is the "best option" for your pet. Always make sure to be easy on yourself, because this is going to be one of the hardest things you do regardless of how well you prepare.

ACTIVITY: A POEM FROM YOUR PET

Read this poem from the point of view of your pet. Through your pet's eyes, you may be able to process the loss more effectively. Try writing your own poem, or just a response, to your pet. Make sure you remind them of all the happy memories you had together when they weren't in pain. What are some of the things you wish you could have said at the end? List things you'd tell your pet if they were here right now. If you're looking for forgiveness, then ask for it. It doesn't even have to be a poem. I promise that you'll feel much better once you've gotten this weight off your chest.

THE LAST BATTLE

If it should be that I grow frail and weak
And pain should keep me from my sleep,
Then will you do what must be done
For this - the last battle- can't be won.
You will be sad I understand,
But don't let grief then stay your hand,
For on this day, more than the rest,
Your love and friendship must stand the test
We have had so many happy years,
You wouldn't want me to suffer so.
When the time comes, please, let me go.
Take me to where to my needs they'll tend,
Only, stay with me until the end
And hold me firm and speak to me
Until my eyes no longer see.
I know in time you will agree
It is a kindness you do to me.
Although my tail its last has waved,
From pain and suffering I have been saved.
Don't grieve that it must be you
Who has to decide this thing to do;
We've been so close—we two—these years,
Don't let your heart hold any tears.

4

THE TENDER ACHE OF LOVE
AND LOSS

"Grief, I've learned, is really just love," says Jamie Anderson. *"It's all the love you want to give, but cannot. All that unspent love gathers up in the corners of your eyes, the lump in your throat, and in that hollow part of your chest. Grief is just love with no place to go."*

THE DAY BULLET LEFT THIS WORLD

Finding the right words to begin this chapter was difficult. I went through several drafts before I could accurately describe to you the emotions I felt the day that I lost Bullet. There are not enough words in my arsenal to express what it felt like to be there with him as he passed away. Bullet's death was very sudden, so I can't emphasize enough how important it is to enjoy every possible moment with your companion. There was a weekend after his eighth birthday where we decided to do a small trip to Bend, Oregon. The day before we left, I had noticed Bullet was eating a little slower than usual. His appetite seemed to be gradually disappearing, so we made a mental note to take him to the vet once we returned from Oregon. Since he was still running around alongside our boxer, Hunter, we thought that he might just have a stomach bug. However, once we got to Oregon, his appetite had decreased even more and he continued to eat slowly.

I did a personal inspection of his entire body, pressing down lightly on all of the areas I thought could be bothering him, but nothing seemed to be wrong on the surface. We continued to have a nice weekend with our friends and family, sitting around the fireplace during the evenings, and walking the boundary of the beautiful golf course that surrounded the Sunriver Resort with Hunter and Bullet in tow. We enjoyed our long weekend, never knowing that it would be Bullet's last vacation with us. When I arrived home on Sunday evening, I could tell that something was still wrong. I picked my sweet boy up and put him in the car to take him to the pet emergency clinic. I had no idea that I wouldn't be bringing him home with me. One day, I'd like to finally bury this guilt I lug around on my shoulders for not giving Hunter a chance to say goodbye to his best friend. I wish I could have known sooner that this was Bullet's last day.

The vet was able to identify what was wrong with Bullet fairly quickly. He had some masses in his stomach and his spleen, and one of them had burst, causing Bullet to bleed internally. We were told that we could send him into surgery immediately and they would try to remove his spleen, as well as the other associated masses. This would hopefully stop the bleeding, and Bullet could make a full recovery. However, without getting a look inside, they couldn't be sure how far the masses had spread. We opted to try the surgery immediately, so they asked us to go home and assured us they would contact us with more information after the procedure. The doctor was so kind, and he brought Bullet out to the lobby to say goodbye before going into surgery. I looked into Bullet's eyes, and I could tell that he knew we were potentially saying goodbye for good. He leaned into me as I hugged him closely. We filled him up with words of positivity and encouragement to try to make him feel better. He was such a tough boy. I still can't help but shed a tear when I think of what I said to him in that moment:

"It's okay if you can't do it, buddy," I said, "I understand and love you either way. But I'll be waiting for you."

A couple of hours later—around midnight—we got a call from the clinic. They told us that the masses had spread into other areas of his stomach and that they wouldn't be able to stop the bleeding. Just one week ago, I would never have imagined I'd be up this late receiving news as devastating as this. Four short days, and Bullet's health had taken a sharp turn for the worst. Now, we were never again going to go on our long walks around the neighborhood, or share a laugh at the park. I sat there in shock for what seemed like an hour.

Our boxer, Hunter, was about three years younger than Bullet. He looked up to Bullet like he was his big brother. We could tell that Hunter was impacted by the loss of Bullet almost as much as we were. Without his best bud around, it took a while for him to start enjoying life again. I had to go out of my way to bring excitement back into his day-to-day routine. Yes, pets absolutely do grieve the loss of their companions.

The days after losing your beloved pet are undoubtedly the hardest. There's just no way to sugar coat that. Looking back, I'm so glad that we all got that last weekend in Oregon to relax and be happy with one another. I'm also glad that I was able to get to know Bullet, and that I had a strong support system to help me through the grieving process after losing him. We had a few really amazing years together before he left this world. It can be extremely difficult to look past those final moments to see all the happy stuff that came before. But it is important to recognize that their experience on this earth doesn't just boil down to those last—likely painful—moments here. Their life was long, beautiful, and full of light. You just have to get past that dark cloud in your brain trying to keep you down.

UNDERSTANDING THE GRIEF OF LOSING A PET

Pets enhance our lives and bring light and joy, even when we're unable to find it anywhere else. That's why it can be so hard to lose your beloved companion. There's no instruction manual on how to grieve, but you can get a better understanding of this process so that you can cope properly without self-destructing. The research we have on grief is vast and still ongoing. Scientists, psychologists, and sociologists all want to better understand why we go through this unnerving process and how we can better cope with these emotions. First, it's important to note that no matter what research is out there, the way that you grieve is completely up to you—so long as it's not counterproductive to your own health. What we can say with confidence is that grief tends to separate into five distinct, nonlinear phases before it is fully realized and accepted. I'd argue that pet owners go through six.

Before being able to feel or process any of the classic stages of grief—denial, anger, bargaining, depression, and acceptance—I think that pet owners often experience a great deal of shock. Feeling shocked when someone passes isn't a new concept, but what researchers don't talk about is the feelings of numbness and detachment that you can feel leading up to their passing if you've had to come to terms with euthanizing your beloved pet to end their suffering. Shock can have some unique effects on the body and the mind. You may choose to shut everything out and avoid all of the things that remind you of your old pal. Or, you may just want to cry for hours on end while holding their favorite toys. There is such a broad range of reactions when it comes to pet loss, so it can be hard to study, and even more difficult to coach someone through (Koening, 2022). What's important is that you remain self-aware as you work through these stages.

People often use denial to cope with the initial shock they're feeling after their pet has passed away. It's a defense mechanism that can ease those overwhelming feelings and put you back into a mindset where you feel safe and comforted by the memories of your pet (Koening, 2022). But denial is counterproductive. Instead of being a step forward in the grief process, denying your true emotions and getting lost in your "grief brain" is a step backward. Then, when someone you don't see that often comes along and asks excitedly about how your pet is doing, you feel devastated all over again when you have to face reality and tell them your beloved pet is dead. We know that deep down, you don't really think your pet is coming home. When you linger in that state where you can *almost* make yourself believe that your companion will be coming around the corner any moment, though, you set yourself up to be disappointed every time. Denial is confusing and somewhat comforting. Some people claim that they see their pet all over the house after they've passed on, but it's not a mindset that will heal you. It's a mindset you want to escape ("The Stages of Grief...," 2014).

Anger is unique because it arrives at the same time reality does. Once the weight of the situation sets in, it smothers you until you explode. Oftentimes, you'll see people who are grieving take their anger out on those around them. They can push friends away, their family, and veterinarians. Blinded by anger, you might even push away the happy memories with your pet that you once held dear. It's tempting to search for someone or something to blame for this huge loss—even ourselves. Anger will push away all of the other things we might be feeling under the surface, such as sadness and fear ("The Stages of Grief...," 2014). When you begin to feel truly helpless, you might even start to bargain for the impossible. We see people bargain with a higher power, themselves, or even their late pet. Those who are stuck in this stage often feel a tremendous amount of guilt about what they did or did not do for their pet toward the end of their life. "If only I could hear her purr one more time," or

"I'd do anything for just one more day," are common reactions at the North Shore Animal League ("The Stages of Grief...," 2014).

When that sadness below the surface finally breaks through that anger, it feels like a tsunami crashing into your chest. This depression will either push you into your own world or cause you to reach out to others for help. It's going to be dark, and there will be times when it feels like you're physically wounded. Your heart is broken, so it's going to take time to heal just like any other organ in your body. Be patient with yourself, and allow yourself to reach each of these stages whenever you're ready ("The Stages of Grief...," 2014). This process is nonlinear, meaning that you don't have to go from denial straight to anger, then onto bargaining, and so on. Always keep in mind that there isn't a "right" way to grieve. Whatever you're feeling is perfectly normal. If you feel like the denial stage skipped right over you, *great*, that just means that you're already one stage down and ready to take on the others.

Acceptance, the final stage of grief, seems to be the easiest concept to grasp, but in practice, it's the most challenging of them all. Accepting your beloved pet's death can feel like a betrayal. You may want to hold on to that anger for good because you feel like your pet deserved better. I'm here to tell you that accepting the harsh reality is the greatest gift you can give them—not holding onto those negative emotions. When you fully embrace and rejoice in the wonderful life you gave your pet, you can finally give your heart a second to heal and make room for the memory of your companion ("The Stages of Grief...," 2014).

Sometimes, people can't just move through the stages and then go on with their lives by themselves. Some people have to learn new coping mechanisms in order to deal with the loss of their pet. People can have a number of mental and physical health difficulties as a result of their grief. When the consequences of bereavement begin to pop up, we must combat them with coping strategies. According to Margaret Stroebe and Henk Schut's study on Dual Processing Models, there are two coping styles that humans utilize in order to fully process grief. Emotions-focused coping is directed at managing your emotions that result from stress, and problem-focused coping is directed at managing and changing the problems causing you distress in the first place. You need to rely on your emotions-focused coping just as much as your problem-focused coping. This means that you should be regulating your behavior along with your emotions. This can be anything from doing something that you enjoy when you start to feel down to reminding yourself of all the good memories with your pet when those tears start to fall. Being self-aware of how your emotions are impacting your actions will help you get through the grieving process without becoming self-destructive (Stroebe and Schut, 1999). For example, while you take care of the physical demands of grief like burying your beloved pet or arranging their keepsakes on a shelf, you should also focus on trying to keep positive memories at the forefront of your mind rather than the sad stuff.

When we organized Bullet's belongings, we decided to keep a lot of the stuff we sorted through. He didn't play very rough with his toys, so they were still in pretty good shape when our next pups entered our lives. There weren't any medications to throw away, handicap ramps to remove, or future vet appointments to cancel, so the stuff we kept brought only good memories to the forefront of our minds. A lot of the physical demands of grief were taken care of for me, but it was still difficult to keep my spirits up as I wandered aimlessly around the house. I found myself scrolling through old pictures of Bullet and I for hours—just trying to remember that day with him. I'd look through hundreds of photos of him just laying there, or doing some sort of funny face that I just *had* to capture on camera, and I'd smile. I am thankful that I have these joyful memories to pull from, because there are times when I look for a way to fuel my guilt and sadness, but when I try to conjure up some memories to bring me down, all that's there are these wonderful moments with my best pal.

THE WEIGHT OF GUILT

Let's take a closer look at this response we call "guilt." In a study titled "Disenfranchised Guilt—Pet Owners' Burden," Lori R. Kogan and her colleagues examined how pet parents experience guilt. Pet owners tend to assume complete responsibility for their pet's life. This leads them to think that they could have done something to prevent their pal's death. Feelings of guilt may also point you down the "what-ifs" rabbit hole. What if I paid a little more attention to their health? What if I went to the vet more often? These thoughts need to be fought off as best you can. Research has found that guilt can boil over and lead to depression and anxiety. This will lead to more negative behavior, and ultimately, the inability to properly regulate your emotions (Kogan et al, 2022).

You know that unpleasant feeling in your gut when you think your thoughts, feelings, or behavior could be considered "wrong" in everyone else's eyes? That is called guilt. It's associated with negative feelings and a sense of responsibility or remorse (Kogan et al, 2022).I know that you can't help but listen to that voice in your head telling you that you could have done better. This is especially hard when you lose someone as close as your furry friend and beloved companion.

A lot of the research has been done using the same methodologies as those interested in studying the guilt parents feel about their parenting practices. This just goes to show you that your pet is not just a pet; they're family. Thinking that you could have done something differently is a completely normal response. There is a long list of things that pet parents feel guilty for during pet ownership. Overfeeding, underfeeding, not spending enough time with their pet—pick your poison. They know that you did everything in your power to help them maintain the greatest quality of life. Take a moment to consider what they might be thankful to you for during their long life. Overall, you should keep in mind that there is no one forcing you to remain in this state of anger and regret after your pet has moved on from this world.

Try not to focus on the events leading up to your pet's passing too much, either. This definitely won't soften the blow. We can't put ourselves in their shoes—they definitely wouldn't fit— but you can remember that their quality of life was what mattered the most. Challenging your negative thoughts with positive ones will give you a chance to forgive yourself ("If Only...," n.d.). Say you start to think about all of the things you could have done differently while your pet was alive. Challenge these thoughts with positive ones, such as all the times you treated your pet to a good time at the park.

Guilt becomes destructive once it has begun to fester and you feel like you can't stop reliving the loss. If you can't seem to get out of that depressive state, then you need to find new ways to deal with this loss. Try to spend some time alone and really examine your own thoughts. Guilt often hides in repetitive thoughts, so breaking free from these patterns can be a great first step. Choosing to think about something else and distracting your brain is one way to cope when you start to fall into destructive patterns. There isn't anything that you can do to change the past, so you've got to be able to identify and accept these emotions eventually. You might even want to consider seeing a therapist if you need additional grief counselling ("If Only...," n.d.).

Achieving self-forgiveness after the loss of a pet is one of the hardest things you'll have to do. Leave the what-ifs at the door and enter a world of compassion free from shame and guilt. It's difficult to reach this point because you can't just look over and ask your pet if you gave them a great life. Even if they were still here today, the obvious language barrier hinders any chance of getting that confirmation. That's why we're haunted by these questions of "Could I have done better?" The truth is, we all make mistakes. There are probably a handful you could think of right now, but these mistakes don't always have heavy consequences. Even if they do, you just need to remember that accidents happen. Sometimes we mess up, we make the wrong decisions, or we don't know what is the right thing to do. The important part is that we're able to forgive ourselves and enjoy the time we do have with our beloved pets ("How To Achieve Self-Forgiveness...," 2021).

If I decided to include all of the ways I messed up as a dog owner during Bullet's lifetime, we'd have a completely different book on our hands. We are human, and we all make mistakes—and, our pets don't even know what a *mistake* is. In their eyes, we could never do any wrong. That's part of the reason why we feel so bad for ourselves once they're gone. All they ever wanted was to be loved and cared for, and we wish we could do that until the end of time. But their time on this earth is so much shorter than ours, and therefore, that much more precious. We shouldn't overwhelm ourselves thinking about the bad stuff when their short lives were still filled with so much good.

FINDING HEALING

You might be thinking to yourself: *why can't I stop crying?* And, once again, I'm here to tell you that it's okay to cry it out. Let that negative energy flow through and out of you, because if you don't let those tears flow now, it could lead to a more traumatic grief experience in the future. Did you know that when you cry because you're emotional, the tears are produced by the endocrine system? These tears are specifically crafted to promote a feel-good, chemical reaction that can reduce feelings of pain and sadness. That means that when we cry, our hormones allow a release of what's called leucine-enkephalin, a chemical that will remove toxins from the body in an attempt to reduce stress (Clark, 2017). Each time that we let our tears fall, our body is actually working toward healing.

We've looked at the stages the professionals have observed, but as we discussed, there isn't just one way to respond to your grief. It's good to take a look at a few different ways to cope with your grief so that you're more inclined to take a less destructive route. First, don't forget to acknowledge your grief. Give yourself permission to let it show in whatever way necessary. While you're allowing yourself to grieve, don't continue to replay your last moments with your pet. If you find yourself falling deeper and deeper into this pit of grief, try reaching out to those who might have a sympathetic ear. This includes the Pet Compassion Careline, Laps of Love, and hundreds of other online support groups that can provide additional support and counseling. With enough research, you may even find a local support group. Places like Everlife Support Groups and the Association for Pet Loss and Bereavement have different locations across the United States and they meet weekly. If you're religious, you may even want to consider asking if your place of worship offers bereavement support groups for pets ("How to Cope with the Death...," n.d.). Don't forget that you also have friends and family who may have experienced this kind of thing before. It may feel like an isolating experience, and like no one could ever understand the hurt you're going through, but I promise that there are people out there ready to guide you through this experience if you just ask.

You may also want to consider memorializing your pet through a "bereavement ritual" of sorts. We talked a little about the commemorative paw prints, but there are several ways that you can keep the memory of your pet alive. Maybe there is a place in your home, or just somewhere special in mind, for you to keep their ashes. You could also choose to plant a tree or some sort of shrub in memory of your beloved pet. Try writing an obituary for your pet, or writing them a letter containing all of your feelings at this moment. Some people choose to make a memory box with their pet's old collar and favorite toys ("How to Cope with the Death...," n.d.), or you can choose to commemorate your pet as we did and get a custom piece of jewelry made. Whatever you choose to do, take your time with it. Allow all your love—as well as all your grief—to soak into it so that every time you look at it, you're filled with that same overwhelming joy that you had when your pet was still by your side.

If you have children in the picture, it may take a few extra steps to get through this process. You don't want to confuse them by lying, only to have them figure it out eventually on their own. Explaining death to a kid, no matter how old, can be extremely complicated. There isn't a right answer to how you should support your child during the loss of their beloved pet. Everyone will have their own unique response to such a trau-matic event, so it's best just to be as prepared as you can be. Be ready to discuss the cycle of life with your child. Try to help them understand that this is just a natural part of life that can't be prevented. Be as gentle as you can while also being informa-tive. Maybe you want them to understand the kind of end-of-life care your pet needed, and to know that you all did everything you could for them. Try to keep these conversations as open as possible. Don't make this a lecture about death. Instead, it should be a discussion on why life is to be celebrated at all times. Life is precious, and you should try to explain to your child that this is why it hurts so much after they've left us (Holloway, 2023).

I'm sure we've all had an experience where our parents told us that our beloved pet went to "live on a farm" or they "ran away" while we were at school. This is not a helpful way to tell children their pet has moved on. It just pushes off the inevitable for someone else to deal with in the future. I'm just saying, you can't be too surprised when you get a call from their teacher saying someone told your kid their pet was dead, not on a farm. Now you've got a grieving child on your hands. Being honest after their pet dies is hard, but it gives them a chance to say goodbye and make peace with it the same way you did (Holloway, 2023). You may even want to try involving your kids in the bereavement ritual. Have them do some artwork for their pet, or let them help you make a commemorative scrapbook. Getting them active and involved will also help them with the grieving process—not just for them, but for you, too. By getting the whole house laughing and reminiscing on all the good times with your old pal, you'll simultaneously brighten the mood and get everyone moving along this journey through grief. In no time at all, everyone will be smiling and sharing their favorite memories with their late pet.

I have a million funny stories to tell about the shenanigans Bullet and I got up to on our morning walks, but it was so heartwarming to hear the stuff my husband missed about Bullet's presence, too. I strongly recommend that you talk to the people in your pet's life and listen to what they have to say, even if they only knew them through you. These memories will heal you in ways you never thought possible. We had an old friend visit not too long after Bullet passed, and when she heard the news, she started to cry. We had no idea that she'd even been that fond of Bullet in the first place, but after a while, she opened up about how much of an impact Bullet had on her when he was first introduced to the family. She wasn't a big "animal person," but she'd come over from time to time for dinner or a movie and Bullet would lay across her lap like he was a lap dog. We always told him to get down, but she'd just shrug and say "guess he lives here now." Apparently, that is what motivated her to find her own pet companion a few years down the line. When she shared this with us, we were all a mess —crying tears of joy because our sweet boy had touched the lives of so many, and his influence would live on in us all.

THROUGH YOUR PET'S EYES

Time to look back through your pet's eyes once again:

Hi there, friend. I know you're missing me a lot right now, but I want you to know that it's okay. Whatever is making your eyes so wet right now, just let it go. You couldn't have controlled what happened to me. I had so much fun with you during my time on this bright, loud, and smelly planet. I couldn't have asked for a better giant to get paired with.

You should know, I lived every moment to the best of my abilities. I smelled every single smell there could possibly be, and I never once thought about what happened ten minutes ago, or what five minutes in the future would look like for me. I was there, in every single moment, soaking up that big smile on your weird, half-hairless face, waiting for the next big thing we were about to do. Of course, I miss our big backyard, and the way the house smelled on Taco Tuesdays—I even miss running away from the vacuum in terror—but I wouldn't change a thing about the life we shared. If I can share anything with you from here, it's to try and be more like that; don't live in those sad moments. Instead, live for me.

I want you to honor me in the way you live from here on out. Take care of yourself. Be as kind to yourself as you were to me. Remember all of the warm, happy memories we had together. Maybe you could use a journal or something to write down all our stories and moments where we made each other laugh. You could plant me a tree, or paint me a picture, to keep me with you for longer. Most importantly, I want you to take care of yourself. Go to the spa for me, will you? I remember you used to scratch my head with those super strong and colorful nails, so go get those done too.

Take a break from the grief, Mom and Dad. It's too unfair for you to miss me this much. I promise you that I am okay. Instead of getting stuck here in this sadness, try to educate other pet parents about how they can avoid feeling so lost and alone. You'll not only honor me, but you'll save lives. I will always love you.

ACTIVITY: TIME TO BE MINDFUL

Part of getting through your grief is being mindful of your thoughts and feelings. It's only natural to want to avoid these painful emotions. A lot of people will alter their reality by simply denying themselves the ability to feel all those emotions that tag along with grief. By being mindful of our feelings, we can learn from these painful emotions and be better prepared to experience all that life has to offer without reverting to our avoidance tendencies. Expressing our emotions honestly and accurately can help us be mindful and work through our grief ("Mindfulness for Grief," n.d.). Take a second to journal whatever comes to mind when you read the following prompts:

- Today I am missing…
- The hardest part of the day is…
- How losing my pet changed me…
- When I think of my pet, I…
- I choose to remember my pet by…
- Some ways I can be kinder to myself are…

____

____

____

____

____

____

____

____

____

____

5

GENTLE WHISPERS OF MEMORY

"When someone you love dies, and you're not expecting it, you don't lose her all at once; you lose her in pieces over a long time —the way the mail stops coming, and her scent fades from the pillows and even from the clothes in her closet and drawers," says John Irving in A Prayer for Owen Meany. *"Gradually, you accumulate the parts of her that are gone. Just when the day comes—when there's a particular missing part that overwhelms you with the feeling that she's gone, forever—there comes another day, and another specifically missing part."*

VISIBLE REMINDERS OF YOUR LOST PET

For a while, it will feel like you can't go anywhere in your home without being reminded of your old pet. Maybe you can't stop tripping over their toys, which are still scattered around the house, or you haven't taken down their leash from the key hooks by the door. Whatever it may be, it's important that you know that these visible reminders can have both a positive and a negative effect on your healing, so it's always important to remain self-aware of how your thoughts and feelings are affecting your behavior. This is one of those moments where you truly need to look inward and figure out what is best for you. Sometimes, these objects can feed an emotional behavior that will keep you stuck in your grief. If you're aware of the fact that their old belongings trigger something inside of you that you can't overcome, then it could be time you pack up some of those belongings and store them somewhere safe. However, most of the time, these objects can link you to your beloved pet and make it feel like a part of them is still around. Something you might ask yourself while sorting through their belongings is "Does this object help me honor my loved one?" If the answer is no, then it's probably time to donate those toys, or pass them on to another bundle of joy who needs them more (Peterson, 2021).

It's important that you recognize whether keeping these items is healing you or hurting you. In order to properly heal, you should be able to decide what reminders you want to keep around and what it's time to cut ties with. At first, we like to set the items aside and give ourselves time to heal. Since we're a multi-pet household, however, we have always kept most items and reused them after a certain amount of time. As life goes on, the heartbreak turns into reminiscing, storytelling, and laughter. You'll smile as you clip the collar on another four-legged best friend. I like to think of it like *The Sisterhood of the Travelling Pants*, but in this case, it's the travelling *collar*.

DEALING WITH THEIR BELONGINGS

Saying goodbye to your loved one who has died is not easy. Getting rid of their stuff might feel like you're trying to get rid of *them* completely. The question we often struggle with the most is how soon is too soon when considering decluttering after the death of your loved one? The most important thing to keep in mind is that everyone is different, and you should never feel pressured to go through their belongings until you're ready. Throwing yourself into this task too soon could have a negative effect on your mental health, and it may even prolong the grieving process. Be sure that you're also aware of how having that stuff hanging around can impact you negatively. If there are negative memories attached to a particular item, this can be even more damaging to your psyche. Say you had to take care of your pet through a merciless cancer or some other injury and you've still got a giant bed spread out on your bedroom floor and a bunch of veterinarian-prescribed pill bottles all over the place. These items could remind you of those painful last moments over and over again, so these should be the first to go (Wheaton, 2020).

Overall, it will be difficult to decide what you'd like to do with your late pet's belongings, so make sure that you're doing a lot of self-reflection and contemplation in terms of what would honor their memory. Some people have reported not being able to ever get rid of those belongings because it would cause even more guilt, and others have experienced this feeling of guilt after throwing out too many of their belongings. There is no shame in taking your sweet time. I mean, take a look at Queen Victoria after her husband, Prince Albert, died in 1861. For 40 years following his death she wore black, and she even had the servants lay his clothes out for him each morning. They also left him a bowl of hot water for shaving. I'm not saying this is the route you should take—in fact, I'd actively advise against mourning your beloved pet for the next four decades—but it just goes to show you that everyone grieves differently (Mendoza, 2021). When you do decide it's the right time, start by decluttering the least sentimental stuff. Try asking your friends, neighbors, or even your coworkers if they would like any belongings that you feel comfortable parting with. You could also consider donating some of those items to second-hand shops. You should absolutely keep the things that make you feel closer to your old pet, but a lot of the time, people feel a weight being lifted after the constant reminders are gone (Wheaton, 2020).

There is no denying that parting with your late pet's belongings is a deeply emotional experience. You should expect to feel powerful waves of emotion as you sort through this stuff. It seems almost cruel to have to deal with this task on top of everything else. But in order to move on eventually, you can't be constantly haunted by memories of pain and grief. Maybe instead of trying to do this alone, you could enlist the help of a friend or family member. That way, you aren't more inclined to make decisions you might regret later—like throwing something out, or giving everything away just to be done with it—

just because you're feeling overwhelmed. You could have a few friends come over just to keep you company along the way. Instead of drowning in all these memories that come flooding back with each toy, food dish, or litter box, you and your friends could reminisce over these fond memories and even share a laugh or two. Your friends can steer the conversation from sad to joyful, despite the heavy weight that hangs over all of you in that moment. You might even want someone else to handle specific things that could trigger more painful memories for you, like clearing out their old bed, cage, or ditching the medications lazily thrown in your junk drawer (Kay, 2021). And hey, who said you have to do it all in one day? Don't forget to take the time you need to grieve properly, and decluttering does not mean that you no longer care. Your pet will always be a part of you, even after you've let yourself move past this pain.

THE ABSENCE OF YOUR PET'S PRESENCE

Going through Bullet's belongings was one of the toughest things I've done. It seemed like every item increased my grief and made that black hole of pain deeper and deeper. I shuffled through every collar, every toy, and every chewed up sock hidden in the yard. Those memories all came rushing back as I handled each item with care. As my family and I navigated the depths of grief and loss, we honored the life of our beloved Bullet every step of the way. Our entire routine was shot after he passed. I would wait for that moment when Bullet would step on the back of my ankles as we got ready for our morning walk, only, it never came. That hurt like hell. Bullet was the protector of the house, but he was also my best friend. He was always by my side, and while he may have looked intimidating to the average onlooker, the most damage he would do was leave a trail of slobber across your face.

Oftentimes, people report that dealing with the loss of routine is the hardest part. Remember that this is a completely normal feeling. You didn't just lose your pet. You lost the life that you both shared together ("Loss of Routine," n.d.). For a few weeks after Bullet passed, I would wait for him by the door before heading out for my walk. Hunter would poke his head up from the couch as if to say "I can come if you want?" That always made me smile a little. It took a while for me to feel comfortable talking about my feelings, but now I truly understand the importance of reaching out to someone—whether a friend, or a pet bereavement service—because not everyone understands how painful it can be. These services recommend that you create new routines to adapt to this feeling of loss in your day-to-day life ("Loss of Routine," n.d.). I decided to switch up my walking route so I didn't have to pass by Bullet's favorite spots each morning.

Some people even recommend bringing a new pet into their home. Deciding to bring home a new furry friend is completely up to you, and it isn't everyone's cup of tea. However, bringing a new friend into the picture can help you maintain your routine and take the focus off of your pain just a little. It won't eliminate your grief, but it can provide a sense of comfort and give you something positive to divert your energy to. If you don't feel ready to adopt a new pet, there are always places where you can volunteer to walk and care for dogs such as a local shelter or SPCA ("Loss of Routine," n.d.).

MOVING FORWARD WITH LOVE

I still don't know if this was a coincidence or not, but Bullet passed away around the same time that we introduced a new arrival in the house. Well, make that two new arrivals. Tiger, the Golden Retriever, and Stormy, the German Shepherd, fell into our laps just two days after we received Bullet's ashes. We've always been a dog family, so the plan to add more fur babies to our pack was already in motion by the time we found out about Bullet's condition. Tiger and Stormy were the rascals we didn't know we needed. It was really hard, and a lot of the time, we felt guilty bringing new puppies into the family as we worked through our grief. But their presence became therapeutic over time. They brought unending joy and laughs, and together, they made up all of the best parts of Bullet. It was like his spirit was reborn in them; like he asked them to stay behind and watch over his family.

As they grew older and developed their own personalities, those faint traces of Bullet were still there. In fact, they only got more prominent over time. It was comforting thinking that those were pieces of Bullet that he left behind for us. He knew what it would take for our hearts to heal, and this was his last gift to us. A last gift from our first and best boy, Bullet.

We try to honor our beloved pal in everything we do. We created custom jewelry pieces with Bullet's ashes, and it has become a tradition ever since. My husband's black bullet casing with the name *Bullet* etched into the side still hangs from his rear-view mirror in the truck. That way, Bullet can still take car rides with us every single day. He loved nothing more than riding in the truck with his dad because he would let Bullet sit up front with all the windows down. We also have our commemorative paw print leaning against a mirror on our bedroom dresser. That way, we can see Bullet each morning as we get ready for the day. Whatever you choose to do in order to cope is up to you, and I promise that you won't regret honoring your best friend in some way, no matter how big or small.

A lot of people say that they don't plan on getting a new dog, but those same people have reported that finding a new furry companion snuck up on them during their darkest hour. There was a man who shared his story online after losing his beloved dog Walter in 2019. He said that Walter's death took a toll on him that he could "probably never convey to someone." He swore he would never have another dog again. He couldn't bear the pain of losing another friend. But just seven months later, he met Akita. She was a "magnificent rescue" who needed him. That man said Akita demanded his love and this helped him heal. Opening his heart when he didn't think it was possible was the key to moving past his grief (BlackPhillip4Eva, 2021).

There is a lot of healing potential behind getting a new pet. You shouldn't feel guilty for doing something that will help you get that pep back in your step. Remember how we talked about that loss of routine that affects people who have lost family? Well, getting a new dog will give you a new routine to stick to. You should try to avoid thinking of your new furry companion as some sort of "replacement" for your late pet. Judy Desmond said it best: "A dog is the only thing that can mend a crack in your broken heart." Each of our beloved pets serve us perfectly in the season. There isn't a "right" time to get a new pet, because everyone's experience with loss is different. If you are considering a new addition to the family, you should make sure that you've worked through a good bit of your grief, and that you're able to move on in a positive way without dwelling on your loss. Trying to fill that paw print-sized hole in your heart too soon never works, because there will never be another pet exactly like your old pal. You can't expect another pet to be able to fill those particular shoes, so if that's what you're hoping for, it's a sign that you're not ready for a new pet.

There is no doubt that a new pet fills that void that your old companion left, but that's not the only potential benefit of bringing home a new pal. On top of preventing loneliness, a new dog can bring purpose and structure back to your daily life. There are also hundreds of dogs stuck in shelters waiting to be brought into a loving home. You should go around to a few places so that you're sure that you're ready, and that you've made the right decision. A lot of people—like our family—have reported finding a pet that is truly special; one that was put in their path for a reason. When you're ready to open your heart to a new bond, make sure you take your time to find the right fit for you. Rest assured that there are plenty of good times ahead ("Urns & Memorabilia," n.d.). Annette McGivney, author of *Pure Land*, says that when she was looking for a new dog, she was "taken back to some of the darkest days" of her childhood. She struggled with this idea that she was somehow "replacing" her old dog Sunny by looking for a new dog. But one fateful night, while she was scrolling through shelter catalogues on her phone at two in the morning, she found Trudy. Trudy was also a victim of abuse, and when Annette read her story, she knew that she had to rescue her (McGivney, 2022). But it was Trudy who rescued Annette.

Overall, you should only move on once you're ready, because taking on a new pet just to fill that void can lead to some potential downfalls if you're not careful. You shouldn't be looking for a new pet to help you "forget" the death of your old pet (Lee, 2022). If you're not really ready to move on, you might end up projecting your negative emotions onto your new companion. If they don't behave like your old pet, you might even begin to resent them in some way. You must be emotionally prepared before you bring in a new addition to the family, so take the time to properly grieve your loss instead of rushing into anything. You may also want to consider talking to everyone else in the house about your idea, because your partner—or even your kids—may not be too keen on the idea of getting a new pet just yet. If you have other animals in the house, they may or may not be ready for a new pal in the house either, so make sure you take into account how territorial your surviving pets may be. Remember how we talked about other pets grieving their lost friends? You need to make sure you're showering your fur baby with extra love now that they're all alone ("When Is It the Right Time…" n.d.). Be sure that you also remind yourself what is involved in owning a new pet before you devote your energy to adopting (Holloway, 2023). A man shared his honest feelings about adopting a new dog after losing his "heart dog" to demonstrate to other grieving pet parents the importance of being self aware:

"Now that he's gone, I do miss having a dog so much, but I'm just not emotionally ready, plus, I'm nervous at the idea of unfairly comparing every dog I look at to him, or expecting nothing less than that intense connection again, which is unfair," he said (InkedAlchemist, 2021). "I'm putting all my trust in the fact that I'll know when the time is right for me to open up my heart again. Concentrating on your healing and self care at the moment is the best thing I can recommend."

There are a few signs that show you might be ready to introduce a new pet into the family. First, if you've given yourself the appropriate time to mourn your loss, then you've probably already begun to feel that pain in your heart dulling. If you've accepted the loss of your late companion, and you can think of your old pal without focusing on the sad stuff, then you're probably ready to move on. That means you're not hearing that little devil on your shoulder saying this is some sort of betrayal, and you're not weighed down by this guilt ("Urns & Memorabilia," n.d.). Don't let this guilt keep you from finding joy again. There's a brilliant quote on an online forum discussing ways to find the strength to welcome in a new friend after the death of your old one from a woman who has lost a few dogs over the years:

"Why wouldn't they want us to be happy with another dog, ya know? We aren't replacing them," she said (1cecream4breakfast, 2021). "There will always be three holes in my heart. One shaped like Sven, one like Ziggy, and one like Lola. As I raise more dogs and have to say goodbye to them, I'll have more holes in my heart. The holes get smaller over time but never fully go away. But my heart still has plenty of love to give to another dog each time."

I like to believe that none of our lost companions want to see us heartbroken and grieving. Though there may never be a *perfect* time to get another pet while grieving a loss, I believe that our late companions want us to have new companionship and see us happy as they look down on us. When Bullet looks down at us playing with Tiger and Stormy, he isn't sad or angry. I think he's probably up there jumping around as if he were right there beside us. He's probably barking at Tiger for playing a little too rough with the tug-of-war toy, or shaking his head at Stormy for peeing on the carpet. I also imagine he's always got a bag of sandwiches at his disposal. No matter what he's up to up there, I know that he is just glad that I've stopped crying over his commemorative paw print (because one more tear and it would've revived the clay and swallowed up the paw print altogether). He's happy that we have opened our hearts and moved forward with love.

We are so lucky to have had a dog as inspiring and impactful as Bullet. He changed our lives in so many ways, which is one of the reasons why it was so hard to move on. A few people saw me taking in Tiger and Stormy as a sign of disrespect—as if I hadn't been affected by Bullet's loss at all. This just wasn't the case. Sure, there are plenty of reasons to not get a new pal after losing one, but there are also several benefits in doing so. We didn't plan for it to work out this way—in fact, most people don't. I think that a piece of me is still grieving the loss of my beloved Bullet, but I know that there is power in the healing process, and even more strength in overcoming this pain. I also know that Bullet wouldn't want me hurting for too long. He would be proud to see how far I've come.

SELF-CARE DURING THE ADJUSTMENT

These overwhelming feelings of loneliness that come with grief could set you on a self-destructive path if you aren't careful. Navigating through this adjustment period can be isolating. But, while it may seem impossible to shift the focus from your pain to your healing, it's absolutely essential. Taking care of yourself during this dark period in your life will demonstrate strength. The hardest part of moving on for me was getting used to Bullet not being the noisiest thing in the house. I used to "hear" Bullet in the other room skidding across the floor and hopping around with the other dogs. When I would go check on them, they'd all stare up with curious eyes as I scanned the room in disbelief. It took a lot of self-reflection and a good amount of concrete, physical self-care to break this habit.

According to UF Small Animal Hospital, College of Veterinary Medicine, there are a couple of different ways to target your grief through self-care. By nurturing not just your emotional state, but your physical, cognitive, and spiritual well-being as well, you can better deal with the heavy waves of emotion that come with grief. Taking care of yourself emotionally means you acknowledge your grief and allow it to be expressed in a healthy manner. Maybe you're journaling each day, or writing letters to your late pet. Whatever it may be, nurturing your emotional well-being is essential to the self-care process.

Your physical condition can be taken care of in a number of different ways. Eating healthy foods and getting a proper amount of exercise is a great place to start. Always ensure that you're getting enough sleep, and try to avoid using substances to numb your pain. Cognitive functioning can be impaired by grief, so make sure that you're stimulating yourself intellectually during this process as well. Cognitive abilities that can be affected include memory and concentration, so try to remain focused on productive things like educating yourself on topics that can help you understand what you're going through. That means picking up this book was also a good place to start. But don't forget about other resources like support groups, family members, and close friends who are there to support you no matter what.

Finally, your spiritual well-being involves keeping yourself connected to what makes you, well, *you*. I'm not saying you need to find religion after your pet dies, but see to it that you don't lose touch with your philosophy on life. A few ideas to get you started include taking a long walk to be with your thoughts, calling a friend you haven't talked to in a while, go get a massage or a pedicure, or do some meditating. There's an endless list of things you can do to be kind to yourself and to those around you to refuel that same energy and excitement for life that you had before ("Self-Care During the Grieving Process," n.d.).

It's not uncommon for people to suffer financially during their late pet's end-of-life care. Surgeries, medications, and constant trips to the vet can be devastating to your wallet, but we do it anyway, because our pets are worth it. However, on top of preparing emotionally, you should also take the time to recover financially before you adopt another pet so that you're ready to be the kind of caretaker you want to be once again. In an online forum, someone shared that it took them a couple of years to adopt again. They wanted to be able to "afford to provide unconditionally for a new pup's needs," so they took the necessary time to heal and build up a foundation for their fur baby. Once they recovered financially, and were prepared to provide care once again, they realized just how many incredible dogs there were out there waiting for their forever home (theknuckular, 2021).

Overall, you have to do what is best for you as you work through your grief. Take care of yourself physically, and nurture your mental health at every step of the way. It won't kill you to take a few days off work to take a trip to refuel your soul. If you're not in a good place financially, then start with the little stuff. Cook yourself something you've been craving, watch a movie that you know makes you happy, or spend some quality time with the people who bring you joy. If you're having a hard time figuring out what makes you happy, talk to someone who can help. See a therapist, call an old friend, or maybe just take a moment to look inward. Self-care doesn't have to be mani-pedis and a trip to the spa. When Bullet passed, I was too sad to take our morning walks alone. For a while, I would just wake up and go to work without that daily release. When I realized that I needed to take care of myself in order to properly move past my grief, I began my morning walks once more. That was my way of continuing to take care of myself through the grief.

ACTIVITY: HONORING THEIR MEMORY

Take a second to think about all the incredible things your pet left behind. This can be joyful memories, physical belongings, or even just how they impacted your life. Did you keep your pet's collar? Maybe their name tag? Were there any fond memories your pet left you to reminisce on forever? How did your pet change your emotional well-being? Write down some of these things so that you can continue to honor their memory without dwelling on the sad stuff.

6

FOREVER WITH YOU IN SPIRIT

"Things we lose have a way of coming back to us in the end," JK Rowling said in her book Harry Potter and the Order of the Phoenix, "if not always in the way we expect."

UNCONDITIONAL LOVE ACROSS DIMENSIONS

I know I've said this before, but just because your pet is gone, it doesn't mean they cease to exist. They live on in a lot of ways in your mind, heart, and soul. Your pal will never truly be gone because they live on in spirit every day. Remember that special bond we discussed in Chapter One? Well, that feeling transcends the bounds of physical distance. You know your pet will forever be in your heart because nothing—not even death—can separate you.

Some people even report feeling connected to their beloved pet beyond the grave. Without the same comfort from your furry companion, you might start reaching for a connection between life's subtle coincidences and your pet's presence. We can never really understand why these things happen, or what kind of message they would be sending us anyways, but it's comforting to think that maybe our pets are out there looking after us. You might be skeptical at first, but Sarah Kessler identified at least twenty different claims from pet parents who believe their pet has tried to communicate with them from beyond (Kessler, 2022).

First, familiar sounds are by far the most common sign that pet parents report after their bundle of joy passes away. Familiar smells are right behind that on the list of things that make it feel like your old furry companion is still hanging around somehow. Memories out of the blue are completely normal, but some pet owners see this as a sign that their pet's spirit could be trying to comfort them. What's worse is when you see or hear your pet's name while you're out in public when you weren't expecting it. Your pulse quickens, and a lump rises in your throat as you glance around the area looking for your old pal. Instead of letting this get you down, think of it as your pet coming to say a quick hello while you're out and about. If you used to sing with your pet, maybe there is a particular song that embodies their spirit. When it plays, you feel like they're right beside you once more. Some people even say they can physically feel their pet's presence at times. Cat owners might feel a light brush up against their leg when there's nothing there.

Others say they can feel their pet still breathing down their neck as they eat (Kessler, 2022).

There are also people who have witnessed odd behavior from the other pets in the house and taken it as a sign that their old pal might be present. This is often accompanied by unexplained movement such as a blurry figure in the corner of your eye, or a pillow that keeps getting knocked off the same section of the couch that your late pet used to lay claim to when he was alive (Kessler, 2022). I feel like Stormy and Tiger probably met Bullet's spirit a few times. There were a handful of coincidences that were too unique to not be a sign.

Carl Jung, a Swiss psychologist and writer coined the term "synchronicity" to define the meaningful coincidences of "two or more events where something other than the probability of chance is involved" (Richardson, 2023). Basically, he defined that feeling you get when you "hear" your old pal in the next room only to find one of their old toys laying in some random location after investigating. These weird coincidences that make it feel like your pet is trying to communicate with you from beyond the grave are actually more common than you think.

These events are meaningful because they typically reflect something happening within. It allows you to see how powerful the mind is, and it inspires us to devote our energy to whatever connections our brain has made between the situation at hand and our own personal issues (Richardson, 2023). For example, when I heard Bullet playing in the next room with Stormy and Tiger, it actually felt like he was in there teaching them the ropes and training them to be the best they could be for me. It made me consider how much I was searching for Bullet in my two new bundles of joy, and I had to start recognizing their individuality as pups.

Some people's experiences connecting with their late pet have been even more profound than I could have imagined. Marianne Soucy lost her beloved black and white Manx cat, Rumi, suddenly and tragically. She never got the chance to say goodbye to her fur baby, so when she asked for a sign that Rumi was at peace somewhere, she was elated to get such a grand response. She and her husband went on a spontaneous trip to a park known for its garden-like atmosphere. They were still weighed down by their grief as they approached a cherry tree in full bloom, so much so that they didn't even see it until the magnificent flowers took up every inch of their view. They were talking about Rumi and how they wished they could get some sort of sign when all of a sudden, the trees began releasing their beautiful pink flowers. It was practically snowing flower petals—and not a single gust of wind or breeze in sight. None of the other trees were moving, and they had no doubt it was Rumi reaching out to say farewell the best way he knew how (Soucy, 2012).

Another woman shared anonymously that she often gets visits from her old pets in her dreams. Her father passed away in April of 2021, and before he died, she told him to visit her in her dreams. She's often been able to spend time with her late father in her dreams, and she says that when she sees him "he's even with the dogs." (Anonymous, 2021a). Another woman says that her pup visits her in the form of a yellow butterfly every time she feels down. They seemingly appear "out of nowhere," as if her pup was popping in to say everything will be okay. Now, every time she sees a yellow butterfly, she's overcome with a soothing feeling that brings her out of her funk immediately (PocketHallowFoot, 2021).

While some people look for traits of their beloved pal in their new pets. Others choose to see visits from dragonflies, hummingbirds, and even unique shaped rocks as signs that their pet is still around (aimeesays, 2021). One person said that they dreamed about their pet for weeks after they passed. It was so surreal, and they "didn't care if other people could see him or not," they just ran over and held their dog in their arms and told him how much they missed him. They said "it was incredibly comforting," which is often the response when people talk about these types of dreams (Anonymous, 2021b). Whether it's items popping up in places they don't belong, or a feeling you get when something happens out of the blue, our beloved pets stick around in mysterious ways and can bring us comfort when we need it the most. Though, you don't have to believe in spirits or ghosts to know that your pet is in your heart.

Polly, a writer for *Exemplore,* wrote an article about "spirit pets." She was interested in learning more about this idea that her beloved cat could be visiting her from beyond the grave. Most people will dismiss these feelings immediately. Who would believe in spirit pets if no one has any proof? Most would say that these stories are just a figment of our imagination—another symptom of our "grief brain"—but opening your heart to these experiences actually has healing potential. Polly explained that she had two cats, and after one—Meg—passed away, she continued to feel her little paw prints prance across the sheets at night to lay down with her owner. She'd check to see if it was her other cat coming to comfort her, but nothing was there. Some people refer to this phenomenon as "phantom cat syndrome." Some people feel their late cat rubbing up against their leg, others see them out of the corner of their eye randomly, and each of these unique connections to their pet might not be as uncommon as we previously believed. Polly's mother came to visit shortly after Meg died, and they got on the topic of "spirit pets." Her mother said that she'd been experiencing the presence of a dog sleeping with her at night. Her mother's old dog used to sleep with her every single night, so she knew that this must be her old pal coming to check in (Polly C, 2023).

"It's no wonder that people like me—and you—will happily accept any sign that our bonds have not been broken by death," says Polly in her article for Exemplore (Polly C, 2023). "The 'phantom cat' we feel hopping into bed at night brings us comfort and quiet joy as we drift off to sleep. I only wish it could happen every night."

Even a self-declared "rational" expert like Dr. Michael W. Fox, a British veterinarian and author of multiple books on communicating with spirit pets, says that animals have the ability to manifest themselves in new forms to bring comfort to their old pet parents. These manifestations are "purely auditory or tactile, as when the deceased animal's footsteps are heard, a cold nose is felt on one's leg, or the deceased cat is felt jumping onto the bed" (Polly C, 2023).

Our pets don't want us to be sad after they're gone. Maybe that's why they tend to visit in mysterious ways when we're missing them the most. And even if they never "visit," we hold them close in our hearts until the end of time. You don't erase those paw prints from your heart when you welcome in a new furry friend. You have so much love to give, and when you're ready, there will be plenty of space in your heart to bond with another animal. Your old pal will be smiling down at you the whole time, because they just want to see you find joy again. I know Bullet will always be around because I see him in Tiger and in Stormy. I hear him skidding around on the hardwood floor while the other dogs are rolling around, and I feel him brush up against me from time to time while I get ready for my morning walk. His spirit rests with his mementos on our nightstand, the commemorative paw print on our dresser, and in the necklace that hangs around the rear view mirror of the truck. He's in our hearts, and he's by my side, forever. I'll always miss him, but I'll also always know exactly where he is—and that he is at peace.

RECOGNIZING ALL THE GOOD YOU HAVE

I have a lot to be thankful for. Bullet was the funniest dog I've ever met. From howling in sync with the emergency vehicles racing by to falling asleep sitting up, he always had us laughing. As time passes, it becomes easier to laugh and remember the small things like that. Those moments felt small and insignificant at the time, but now, they serve as unforgettable memories frozen in history. To this day we can't get the puppies to howl alongside the emergency vehicles like Bullet used to, but we sure get a kick out of doing it ourselves when they pass.

I always tell people that Bullet personally picked Tiger just for me because I saw so many pieces of him pop up in Tiger as time passed. I believed it more and more each time a new coincidence would come along. I think Bullet knew that I would need a companion to lie at my feet every day as I worked from home —as he used to do—and he knew that I needed a companion to be by my side in some of my hardest moments that were still yet to come. Tiger was stuck to me like glue as if he'd been trained to do it by my old pal.

Feeling as though your new pet is somewhat connected to your old pet is not an uncommon phenomenon. This brings some people comfort and reassurance, reminding them that their pet is still with them in spirit. A lot of people say that they've seen their new dog mimic their old dog's personality traits as if their old pal is hanging around teaching them the ropes. Some say that it's like their pets met in another lifetime. Other's go as far as to say that their pet's soul was transferred into this new bundle of joy. One woman said that her cat Millie helped guide the greyhound that came into her life unexpectedly after Millie passed in 2013. She didn't understand why her greyhound would "boop" the urn with Millie's ashes in it that sat on her bedside table every single morning. She thought it was cute, but never looked too deeply into it until one day, she decided to look at the details on the urn. Millie passed away on February 2nd, 2013, and her greyhound was born just ten days later on February 12th, 2013. She looked her greyhound in the eyes and said "Millie says hi, huh?" Since then, her greyhound hasn't gone near the urn, as if Millie's mission to deliver the message was complete, and she was now at rest (Kitchu22, 2021).

Having a pet companion will bless you with some of the happiest days you'll ever experience. When they're gone, it might seem like you'll never feel that type of joy again. But under the watchful eye of your pet's spirit, and with the company of your support systems—and even new companions—you will heal and be able to open your heart again. Our lives are guided and dictated by our capacity to love. For some, that's loving your family, your partner, and your children. For others, our hearts go out to our fur babies, and we do everything in our power to love and care for them for the short time they are in our lives. So even if you don't believe in all this "spirit pet" stuff, open your mind to this idea that your pet will always be with you, and take comfort in the fact that your love transcends the limitations of this world. Even if I don't believe in ghosts, I do believe that Bullet still has a lasting impact on our day-to-day lives. I can feel him comforting me when I feel sad, and I can see his sparking personality shining through our other pets' personalities.

ACTIVITY: A FLY ON THE WALL

A classic writing prompt is to write a short story with just one scene but from the point of view of a fly on the wall. We're going to put a little twist on this. Even if you don't believe in it, imagine that your old pal decided to pay you a visit, but they had to embody the figure of something around you. Maybe this is still a fly on the wall, or your washer machine, or even a tree in the backyard. Be as silly and unrealistic as you want, or use this to get a little closure. Did they come to say a proper good-bye? Are they just trying to get one last laugh out of you? Be as serious or as goofy as you'd like, but make sure you touch on why they chose to visit you in specific that moment.

7

A POEM FROM YOUR FAITHFUL COMPANION

"Over the years I've come to appreciate how animals enter our lives prepared to teach," says Nick Trout, *"and far from being burdened by an inability to speak, they have many different ways to communicate. It is up to us to listen more than hear, to look into more than past."*

THROUGH YOUR PET'S EYES

In an attempt to show you how much we meant to our beloved pets, I've written this poem from their point of view. I hope this can put into perspective the kind of enduring love and joy your pet felt in every moment with you. All of those incredible memories you have of your pet? Imagine those again, only this time, from the point of view of your companion who wants nothing more than to show you infinite affection to ensure you remember how much they love you, even after they're gone. Our pets can no longer show us how they feel, but they can love us unconditionally, and that sort of never-ending love is what inspired this piece. It's also what reassures us that our pets are looking out for us, even after they've left this earth.

Hello again, friend.
I know our fun times have come to an end,
but don't you let another tear fall,
because all the times we had were a ball.

Speaking of ball—Do you remember that time at
    the park
when we stayed until after dark?
And we watched the bright orange ball in the sky touch
    the water—
I remember it dipped under the surface, without falter.

I also remember your laughter.
And all the good times thereafter.
I used to love the way you'd rub my belly,
and the way you smelled when you got back from the
    deli.

And to you it didn't matter,
because in the absence of all chatter
gave us all the more time
for stuff photos couldn't capture.

Like all the times we sat in the dark
and the box with moving pictures would make me bark.
But you'd just look at me and chuckle,
rub my head, and then we'd cuddle.

Try to keep these memories in the light—
even if you have to try with all your might
to keep the dark locked deep within.
Don't let this grief win.

When you start to get down
I don't want you to frown—
In fact, I want you to vow
that you'll always live in the now.

Don't dwell on the past—
Hold on to those good memories (and make them last)
Because I was never just a pet;
I'm a part of your life's story that you won't ever forget.

Remember me fondly—
and remember the price of love is costly
But it was worth it to me.
So, open your heart, let go, and be free.

ACTIVITY: A POEM FROM YOUR PET

After reading that poem from your pet, I want you to try and embody your old pal's spirit and give it a try yourself. Whether it be a poem from your old hamster, cat, dog, or turtle, try to be as specific to their story as possible. Jot down a few of your favorite memories together for inspiration. Use the poetic imagery and child-like tone to bring wonder to this experience. Your pet has no idea how long you'll go on to live without them. They don't feel regret for not being able to stick around for a little longer. This poem is going to be useful in showing you how forgiving and loving your late pet was so that you can shed any remaining feelings of guilt or regret.

____

____

____

____

____

____

____

____

____

____

CONCLUSION

"Pets bring vital energy to our homes and lives," says Laura Staley. *"Pets communicate many messages about love and connection. Care tenderly for all pets throughout their precious lives. The interspecies dance of love softens and expands the heart."*

Take a moment to reflect on your journey of healing and growth by reviewing those journal entries I asked you to create at the end of each chapter. A pet's one and only flaw is that its life is too short. We would be here all day if I listed the countless lessons that Bullet taught our family. We learned about love, resilience, and strength. We learned that these qualities outweigh the grief that was caused by his loss. The signs that we see in our everyday life have allowed us to heal and open our hearts again. Our pets' unwavering love allows us to become more and more like them—a perfect best friend.

Always remember that it is normal to still feel those moments of sadness and loss. But it's how you overcome these emotions that defines your healing. Your pet doesn't truly leave you once they're gone. They had such a profound effect on your life, and they'll live on in so many ways. Whether it's in the stuff they left behind, or the memories that you shared, your pet will be with you in spirit. If you followed my advice, then you're probably already surrounded by gentle reminders of your life with your late pet. Maybe their commemorative paw print is placed somewhere you can see it each day, or their name tag hangs on your car keys. You might even choose to continue journaling and writing letters to your late companion to regain that connection you've lost. All of these celebrations of life shouldn't bring you down. Don't forget that they're there to honor your pet's memory, not make you miss them more.

Goodbyes are never easy. If you were present at the moment that your pet left this earth, it sticks with you, and it's difficult to forget. That's why it's important that we let ourselves feel this pain deeply, so we can work on healing the broken parts of ourselves and prepare to move on when the time is right. Bottling up these emotions will cause your pain to seep out in unhealthy ways. Don't forget to let yourself cry if you need to. Remember, crying is a great emotional release that can actually soothe your pain. If you're still struggling to get through your grief, don't be afraid to ask for help when you need it. If you enjoyed the activities I provided, try dedicating some more time to journaling activities. You could write your old pal a million letters until you've said all that there is left to say—nobody is going to judge you. As long as you're working through your grief constructively, and not falling victim to any self-destructive tendencies, then you're on the road to healing and being able to move forward with your life. They may be gone physically, but those memories you have will stay frozen in history forever.

What's even more exciting is that you can call upon these memories whenever you begin to feel down. Remember, try not to harp on the bad stuff. Zero in on those good moments when you both felt on top of the world—indestructible and filled with joy. Share those memories with your friends, your family, and your new furry companions. Whatever you do, just try to live on with love in your heart rather than regret, grief, or despair. We all wish our companions could stay by our side forever. That's why it hurts so bad once they're finally gone. Instead of trying to ignore the pain, use it to learn, heal, and move on from here. It might seem impossible, but you've made it this far. Just keep taking it one day at a time.

Our pet's lives are short, but their influence lives on forever. You will always remember your first pet, and your first loss is going to stick with you as well, but when we open our hearts and homes to an animal, that's the responsibility that we take on. We must carry these pets on in our hearts because it teaches us about life, about loss, and about being able to move beyond your grief. There are plenty of ways to heal the paw print-sized hole in your heart, you just have to open your mind to new experiences. You should never feel afraid or ashamed of asking for help. Pet loss and the grief that accompanies it can be debilitating, but there are plenty of pet parents out there like me who want to help you through this pain and teach you how to move on in a healthy way.

I sometimes forget that there are so many incredible ways to keep Bullet's spirit alive, which is why I decided to share with you all the incredible advice I've collected along my own journey through grief and pet loss. If one of these techniques doesn't work for you, try something else. Not everyone is going to be interested in making custom jewelry, writing letters, or even getting a new companion eventually. That's okay. Everyone experiences grief a little differently, and everyone has their own way of healing those paw print-sized wounds on our hearts. Instead of trying to figure out what's "right" and when you "should" move on, take it easy on yourself and let your heart do the work. Grief can be a long, strenuous battle, but it's a necessary hurdle in life that makes us stronger. It shows us just how precious life is, and how important it is that we open our hearts to love, even after the loss of our beloved pet companion.

EPILOGUE

GOODBYE, MY FRIEND

I know that the doctor gave me time to say goodbye to Bullet before he went into surgery that fateful day, but I wasn't ready to let go at that moment. I feel as though I need to make a proper goodbye to my old pal. Most of the pain we feel after our pet is gone comes from the realization that we won't ever get to talk to them again. To some of us, our pets are our best friends and greatest confidants. Sometimes I find myself making small remarks to Bullet as I get ready in the morning beside his paw print on our dresser. I've even caught my husband clutching his custom jewelry in the truck before he drives off to work or before he comes in from a long day. I know he's not gone from our lives, but this book, and this letter, is my way of finally saying a proper farewell to my beloved Bullet.

* * *

Dear Bullet.

I miss you every day, buddy. I know you sent Tiger and Stormy to take care of us, but they can only help us heal so much. I reached out to family members after you left us because I was so broken up about it. I was angry with the vet, myself, and this earth for blessing me with an incredibly loyal sidekick who only got to live a fraction of the time that I will. It's almost cruel how perfect you were, and yet, taken too soon. But I've learned from this pain one very important lesson: moving on and letting go doesn't mean I'm letting go of you. You still live on in our lives every single day. Each time I grab my clothes in the morning I see your paw print on my dresser. Every car ride feels less lonely with your name tag hanging from the rear-view mirror. My days are less gloomy now that I've opened my eyes to this reality— since I've begun to heal.

Thank you for being a part of my life. Thanks for all the times you made me laugh, all the slobber-soaked kisses, and all the times you cheered me up when all I wanted to do was soak your fur in fresh tears. You were always my best friend and greatest protector. My morning walks, car rides, and days off from work would have been so boring without you by my side. You gave me purpose, and I hope I gave you something equally as special in return. I guess I'll never know exactly how you felt when you left this earth, but I hope that you knew how much I loved you, and how thankful I was for every-thing you gave me. I will never forget all the lessons you taught me, all the good times we had, and all the love we shared. Goodbye, my very best friend. Until I see you next, be a good boy for me, okay?

With all my love,

Ruby

* * *

ACTIVITY: "DEAR OLD PAL,"

This is your opportunity to celebrate your old pal's remarkable life and capture the love they have bestowed upon you. Pour your emotions onto the page as you express gratitude for all the joy they brought and the lasting impact they left on your soul. Send the praises to the heavens, and don't forget to thank them for all they have done for you. Maybe even scold them one last time (jokingly, of course) for ripping up the corner of the couch while you were at work, or for eating the sandwiches you left out in the open (ahem, Bullet, I'm talking about you.). Let the letter serve as a testament to the profound bond you shared and a tribute to the memories that will forever be cherished. Use the space below to compose your letter:

MESSAGE FROM RUBY WOODS

Thank you to all of you who have taken the time to read this book. The Healing Journey of Pet Loss is a compilation of stories and lessons from over the years; writing the book ultimately took me on my own unique path of healing my heartbreak from Bullet. My hope is that this book serves as a resource, guide and comfort for others walking similar journeys. I am overjoyed and thankful for the support I've received with my very first book. If this book has touched your life, given you steps to take toward healing or even a laugh, **please leave a review or share with friends**. I wish you all the very best on your pet loss journey.

All my best until the next book!

Ruby Woods

REFERENCES

1cecream4breakfast. "How to Heal after the Loss of a Pet." Reddit. September, 2021. https://www.reddit.com/r/Petloss/comments/qdg5b2/comment/hhmdso2/?utm_source=share&utm_medium=web3x&utm_name=web3xcss&utm_term=1&utm_content=share_button.

"10 Warning Signs Your Dog Needs to Go to the Veterinarian." Town & Country Veterinarians and

Pet Resort. Accessed August 28, 2023. https://www.tandcvets.com/10-warning-signs-your-dog-needs-to-go-to-the-veterinarian/.

Aimeesays. "For All You Who Have Lost a Dog, Are There Any "Signs" You Saw of Them after They Had Passed?" Reddit. September 26, 2021. https://www.reddit.com/r/dogs/comments/q39ouy/for_all_you_who_have_lost_a_dog_are_there_any/.

Amiot, Catherine, Brock Bastian, and Pim Martens. "People and Companion Animals: It Takes Two to Tango." *BioScience 66*, no. 7 (2016): 552–560. Accessed August 19, 2023. https://doi.org/10.1093/biosci/biw051.

Anderson, Mark. "Ways To Make Your Pet'S Last Day Special." Pets R.I.P. October 13, 2022. https://petsrip.com.au/ways-to-make-your-pets-last-day-special/.

Anonymous. "For All You Who Have Lost a Dog, Are There Any "Signs" You Saw of Them after

They Had Passed?" Reddit. September 26, 2021. https://www.reddit.com/r/dogs/comments/q39ouy/for_all_you_who_have_lost_a_dog_are_there_any/.

Anonymous. "Tell Your Stories of Your Deceased Pets "Visiting" You after Their Passing." Reddit. September 26, 2021. https://www.reddit.com/r/dogs/comments/ocdizd/tell_your_stories_of_your_deceased_pets_visiting.

Asrtaldays83. "LPT: If Your Pet Is Nearing the End of Its Life, Look into At-home Euphenasia." Reddit. December, 2022. https://www.reddit.com/r/LifeProTips/comments/z19fy4/comment/ixae5ls/?utm_source=share&utm_medium=web3x&utm_name=web3xcss&utm_term=1&utm_content=share_button.

Aubrey, Sophie. "More People Are Treating Pets as 'Family Members Who Understand Them'." *The Sydney Morning Herald.* October 24, 2019. https://www.smh.com.au/lifestyle/life-and-relationships/treat-your-fur-baby-as-a-family-member-you-re-in-a-big-club-20191023-p533k0.html.

Ballard, Jamie. "Most Pet Owners Say Their Pets Are Part of the Family." YouGov. December 13, 2019. https://today.yougov.com/topics/society/articles-reports/2019/12/13/how-americas-pet-owners-feel-about-their-furry-fri.

Beautiful-Page3135. "LPT: If Your Pet Is Dying, Be Mentally Prepared to Have Them Humanely Euthanized at the Veterinary Hospital in a Quick Manner." Reddit. March, 2023. https://www.reddit.com/r/LifeProTips/comments/11tejo9/comment/jciwyad/?utm_source=share&utm_medium=web3x&utm_name=web3xcss&utm_term=1&utm_content=share_button.

Beetz, Andrea, Kerstin Uvnäs-Moberg, Henri Julius, and Kurt Kotrschal. "Psychosocial and Psychophysiological Effects of Human-animal Interactions: The Possible Role of Oxytocin." *Front. Psychology 3,* no. 234 (2012). Accessed August 22, 2023. https://doi.org/10.3389/fpsyg.2012.00234.

BlackPhillip4Eva. "How to Heal after the Loss of a Pet." Reddit. September, 2021. https://www.reddit.com/r/Petloss/comments/qdg5b2/comment/hhmtbs8/?utm_source=share&utm_medium=web3x&utm_name=web3xcss&utm_term=1&utm_content=share_button.

Burgess, Julie, and Mindy Waite Ph.D.. "Bucket List: 18 Things to Do Before Putting Your Dog to Sleep." Senior Tail Waggers. January 13, 2023. https://seniortailwaggers.com/things-to-do-before-putting-your-dog-down/.

Burnett-Brown, Dr. Jacqueline Ph.D.. "11 Tips from a Therapist for Grieving the Loss of a Dog After Euthanasia." Senior Tail Waggers. April 11, 2022. https://seniortailwaggers.com/grieving-the-loss-of-a-dog/.

C, Polly. "Spirit Pets: Signs Your Deceased Pet Is Visiting You." Exemplore. May 19, 2023. https://exemplore.com/spirit-animals/pet-spirits-are-they-real.

Clark, Adam. "My Pet Died and I Can't Stop Crying." Psychology Today. Psychology Today, March 12, 2017. https://www.psychologytoday.com/intl/blog/animal-attachment/201703/my-pet-died-and-i-cant-stop-crying.

Corgimatic. "Veterinarians of Reddit, What is the Most Remarkable Example of Intuition Have You Experienced between a Person and Their Pet?" Reddit. August 28, 2016. https://www.reddit.com/r/AskReddit/comments/5t3rxc/comment/ddk70xa/?utm_source=share&utm_medium=web3x&utm_name=web3xcss&utm_term=1&utm_content=share_button.

"Deep Connections: The Power of the Human-Animal Bond." LoneTreeVet. Lone Tree Veterinary Medical CenteR, Accessed August 19, 2023. https://www.lonetreevet.com/blog/human-animal-bond/.

Foospork. "LPT: If Your Pet Is Dying, Be Mentally Prepared to Have Them Humanely Euthanized at the Veterinary Hospital in a Quick Manner." Reddit. March, 2023. https://www.reddit.com/r/LifeProTips/comments/11tejo9/comment/jcl2fpt/?utm_source=share&utm_medium=web3x&utm_name=web3xcss&utm_term=1&utm_content=share_button).

Grandgeorge, Marine, and Martine Hausberger. "Human-animal Relationships: From Daily Life to Animal-assisted Therapies." *Ann Ist Super Sanita* 47, no. 4 (2011): 397-408. Accessed August 19, 2023. https://doi.org/10.4415/Ann_11_04_12.

Grimm, David. "How Dogs Stole Our Hearts: Canines Make Humans Produce More "Trust Hormone," and Vice Versa." Science. April 16, 2015. https://doi.org/10.1126/science.aab2491.

Hicklin, Tianna, and Geri Piazza. "The Power of Pets: Health Benefits of Human-Animal Interactions." News in Health (NIH). Department of Health and Human Services, February 2, 2018. https://newsinhealth.nih.gov/2018/02/power-pets.

Hodge, Kayne. "Denial to Acceptance– What You Need to Know." Mental Health Center. Mental Health Center, June 5, 2023. https://www.mentalhealthcenter.org/denial-what-you-need-to-know/.

Holloway, Sadie. "Adopting a New Pet After Your Cat or Dog Passes Away." Pet Helpful. April 11, 2023. https://pethelpful.com/pet-ownership/Adopting-a-New-Pet-After-Your-Cat-or-Dog-Passes-Away.

Holloway, Sadie. "How to Talk to Children About the Death of a Family Pet." Pet Helpful. April 11, 2023. https://pethelpful.com/pet-ownership/How-to-Talk-to-Your-Children-About-the-Death-of-a-Pet.

"How To Achieve Self-Forgiveness From Pet Loss." Rainbow Bridge Pet Memorials. January 25, 2021. https://rainbowbridgepetmemorials.com/2021/01/25/how-to-achieve-self-forgiveness-from-pet-loss.

"How to Cope with the Death of Your Pet." Humane Society. The Humane

Society of the United States, Accessed September 15, 2023. https://www. humanesociety.org/resources/how-cope-death-your-pet.

"How To Know Whether Your Pet Is Nearing The End Of Life." Viera East Veterinary Center. Accessed August 28, 2023. https://www.vieravet.com/ services/dogs/blog/how-know-whether-your-pet-nearing-end-life.

"Human-animal Bond." AMVA. American Veterinary Medical Association, Accessed August 19, 2023. https://www.avma.org/one-health/human-animal-bond#:~:text=The%20human%2Danimal%20bond%20is,%2C% 20animals%2C%20and%20the%20environment.

Hunter, Tammy. "Quality of Life at the End of Life for Your Dog." VCA Animal Hospitals. Accessed September 5, 2023. https://vcahospitals.com/ know-your-pet/quality-of-life-at-the-end-of-life-for-your-dog.

"If Only…. How to Deal with Pet Loss Guilt." The Ralph Site. Accessed September 15, 2023. https://www.theralphsite.com/index.php?idPage=86.

"Is It Beneficial to Have Other Pets Present During Euthanasia?" Creature Comfort Care. April 29, 2015. https://www.creaturecomfortclinic.com/ blog/2015/4/29/is-it-beneficial-to-have-other-pets-present-during-euthanasia.

Kay, Frances. "Knowing When It'S Time to Get Rid of Their Things." Everlasting Memories. June 1, 2021. https://www.evrmemories.com/knowing-when-it-s-time-to-get-rid-of-their-things.

Kessler, Sarah. "20 Common Claims of Signs From Deceased Pets." Cake. June 8, 2022. https://www.joincake.com/blog/signs-from-deceased-pets/.

Kitchu22. "For All You Who Have Lost a Dog, Are There Any "Signs" You Saw of Them after They Had Passed?" Reddit. September, 2021. https://www. reddit.com/r/dogs/comments/q39ouy/comment/hfqfhf4/?utm_source= share&utm_medium=web3x&utm_name=web3xcss&utm_term=1&utm_ content=share_button.

Koening, Adam. "The Stages of Grief After Losing a Pet." Choosing Therapy. October 12, 2022. https://www.choosingtherapy.com/stages-of-grief-pet-loss/.

Kogan, Lori R., Cori Bussolari, Jennifer Currin-McCulloch, Wendy Packman, and Phyllis Erdman. 2022. "Disenfranchised Guilt—Pet Owners' Burden" Animals 12, no. 13: 1690. https://doi.org/10.3390/ani12131690

Lagoni, Laurel M.S. "Nine Questions to Consider When Planning Your Pet'S End-of-Life Care." Bmorehumane. World by the Tail Inc, 2014. https://

bmorehumane.org/wp-content/uploads/2020/07/Nine-questions-to-consider-when-planning-your-pets-end-of-life-care.pdf.

Lee, Jenna. "Overcoming Guilt About Getting a New Dog After You've Lost One." Jenna Lee Designer Doodles. August 10, 2022. https://www.jennalee doodles.com/post/how-to-overcome-guilt-about-getting-a-new-dog-after-losing-one.

Levy, Julie Ph.D., Kimberly Olson, and Bo Norby. "DNA Studies Reveal that Shelter Workers Often Mislabel Dogs as 'Pit Bulls'." UF Health. University of Florida College of Veterinary Medicine, February 17, 2016. https://www.vetmed.ufl.edu/2016/02/17/dna-studies-reveal-that-shelter-work ers-often-mislabel-dogs-as-pit-bulls/.

"Loss of Routine." The Ralph Site. Accessed September 19, 2023. https://www.theralphsite.com/index.php?idPage=80.

McGivney, Annette. "What I'Ve Learned from Loving a New Dog While Grieving Another." Outside. April 4, 2022. https://www.outsideonline.com/culture/essays-culture/pet-loss-dog-grief-attachment-theory.

Mendoza, Marilyn A. Ph.D. "What Do I Do With My Loved One'S Belong-ings?" Psychology Today. January 1, 2021. https://www.psychologytoday.com/intl/blog/understanding-grief/202101/what-do-i-do-my-loved-one-s-belongings.

"Mindfulness for Grief." Griefline. Accessed September 26, 2023. https://griefline.org.au/resources/mindfulness-for-grief/#:~:text=Healing%20from%20grief%20caused%20by,avoiding%20or%20stopping%20the%20process.

Monahan, Dr. Laura. "How to Emotionally Prepare for the Death of a Pet." Atlantic Veterinary Hospital. June 19, 2022. https://www.atlanticvetseat tle.com/emotionally-prepare-for-the-death-of-a-pet.

"Moving With A Pet: It's Possible!" Sioux Falls Area Humane Society. Sioux Falls Area Humane Society, https://www.sfhumanesociety.com/blog/47/moving19.

MrsNuggs. "LPT: If Your Pet Is Nearing the End of Its Life, Look into At-home Euphenasia." Reddit. December, 2022. https://www.reddit.com/r/LifeProTips/comments/z19fy4/comment/ixd3li3/?utm_source=share&utm_medium=web3x&utm_name=web3xcss&utm_term=1&utm_con tent=share_button.

Murray, Wistar. "Exploring the Deep Bonds between Humans and Their

Companion Animals." Thriveworks. December 15, 2021. https://thrive works.com/blog/deep-bonds-between-humans-companion-animals.

Owczarczak-Garstecka, Sara C., Rosa E. P. Da Costa, Naomi D. Harvey, Kassandra Giragosian, Rachel H. Kinsman, Severine Tasker, and Jane K. Murray. ""It'S Like Living with a Sassy Teenager!": A Mixed-Methods Analysis of Owners' Comments about Dogs between the Ages of 12 Weeks and 2 Years." *Animals 13*, no. 11 (2023). https://doi.org/10.3390/ani13111863.

Pascoe, Alley. "The Fur-Baby Boom: Why Millennials Are Trading Prams For Pooches." Marie Claire. March 4, 2022. https://www.marieclaire.com.au/fur-baby-boom.

"Pet Care Market Size & Share Analysis—Growth Trends & Forecasts (2023 - 2028)." Mordor Intelligence. Accessed August 23, 2023. https://www.mordorintelligence.com/industry-reports/pet-care-market.

Peterson, Reid. "Coping With Sentimental Objects After Loss." Medium. September 20, 2021. https://griefrefuge.medium.com/coping-with-senti mental-objects-after-loss-a0625fa9b6c8.

"Pets and Mental Health." Mental Health Foundation. Mental Health Foundation, Accessed September 26, 2023. https://www.mentalhealth.org.uk/explore-mental-health/a-z-topics/pets-and-mental-health.

"Pets are now Family Members." PFIAA Pet Food Industry Association Australia. Pet Food Industry Association Australia, January 7, 2020. https://pfiaa.com.au/pets-are-now-family-members.

Pierce, Jessica Ph.D.. "Preparing for the Death of a Pet." Psychology Today. March 23, 2021. https://www.psychologytoday.com/us/blog/all-dogs-go-to-heaven/202103/preparing-for-the-death-of-a-pet.

PocketHallowFoot. "For All You Who Have Lost a Dog, Are There Any "Signs" You Saw of Them after They Had Passed?" Reddit. September, 2021. https://www.reddit.com/r/dogs/comments/q39ouy/for_all_y ou_who_have_lost_a_dog_are_there_any/.

"Puppy Development: Stages from Birth to Two Years Old." The Resource Center at Best Friends Animal Society. Best Friends Animal Society, Accessed August 25, 2023. https://resources.bestfriends.org/article/puppy-development-stages-birth-two-years-old.

"Puppy to Senior: A Dog's Stages of Life." Dogsee. Dogsee Chew, February 18, 2022. https://www.dogseechew.in/blog/puppy-to-senior-a-dogs-stages-of-life.

RackaGack. "LPT: If Your Pet Is Nearing the End of Its Life, Look into At-home Euphenasia." Reddit. December, 2022. https://www.reddit.com/r/LifeProTips/comments/z19fy4/comment/ixaotqh/?utm_source=share&utm_medium=web3x&utm_name=web3xcss&utm_term=1&utm_content=share_button.

Richardson, Tanya C. "18 Examples Of Synchronicities & What To Do When They Happen To You." Mind, Body, Green Mindfulness. January 17, 2023. https://www.mindbodygreen.com/articles/synchronicities.

Sabeljax. "Veterinarians of Reddit, What is the Most Remarkable Example of Intuition Have You Experienced between a Person and Their Pet?" Reddit. August, 2016. https://www.reddit.com/r/AskReddit/comments/5t3rxc/comment/ddkc5mm/?utm_source=share&utm_medium=web3x&utm_name=web3xcss&utm_term=1&utm_content=share_button.

Salo, Päivi M. PhD, and Darryl C. Zeldin MD. "Does Exposure to Cats and Dogs Decrease the Risk of Developing Allergic Sensitization and Disease?" *The Journal of Allergy and Clinical Immunology 124*, no. 4 (2009): 751-752. Accessed August 19, 2023. https://doi.org/10.1016/j.jaci.2009.08.012.

Saunders, Jessica, Layla Parast, Susan H. Babey, and Jeremy V. Miles. "Exploring the Differences between Pet and Non-pet Owners: Implications for Human-animal Interaction Research and Policy." *PLoS ONE 12*, no. 6 (2017). Accessed August 22, 2023. https://doi.org/10.1371/journal.pone.0179494.

Soucy, Marianne. "Synchronicity after Pet Loss: A True Story." Healing Pet Loss with Marianne Soucy. 2012. Accessed September 26, 2023. https://healingpetloss.com/synchronicity-after-pet-loss-a-true-story.

"The Stages of Grief – Losing a Pet." North Shore Animal League America. Animal League America, February 25, 2014. https://www.animalleague.org/blog/tips/life-with-pets/stages-of-grief/.

"Self-Care During the Grieving Process." UF Health. Small Animal Hospital College of Veterinary Medicine, Accessed September 19, 2023. https://smallanimal.vethospital.ufl.edu/resources/pet-loss-support/self-care-during-the-grieving-process.

Stroebe, Margaret, and Henk Schut. "THE DUAL PROCESS MODEL OF COPING WITH BEREAVEMENT: RATIONALE AND DESCRIPTION." *Death Studies 23*, no. 3 (1999): 197-224. Accessed September 15, 2023. https://doi.org/10.1080/074811899201046.

Syufy, Franny. "How to Care for Your Cat: Cats Go through Several Phases of

Aging." The Spruce Pets. June 13, 2019. https://www.thesprucepets.com/help-your-cat-live-longer-555004.

Theknuckular. "How to Heal after the Loss of a Pet." Reddit. September, 2021. https://www.reddit.com/r/Petloss/comments/qdg5b2/comment/hhoz2yc/?utm_source=share&utm_medium=web3x&utm_name=web3xcss&utm_term=1&utm_content=share_button.

Trautner, Tracy. "Which Pet Is Right for Me?" Michigan State University Extension. Michigan State University, December 12, 2017. https://www.canr.msu.edu/news/which_pet_is_right_for_me.

"Urns & Memorabilia." Pets in Peace. September 22, 2023. https://www.petsinpeace.com.au/getting-a-new-pet-after-the-loss-of-a-pet-how-to-know-if-youre-ready.

Vormbrock, J K., and J M. Grossberg. "Cardiovascular Effects of Human-pet Dog Interactions." *Journal of Behavioral Medicine 11*, no. 5 (1988): 509-517. Accessed August 23, 2023. https://doi.org/10.1007/BF00844843.

"What Is the Human-Animal Bond?" Habri. The Human Animal Bond Research Institute, Accessed August 19, 2023. https://habri.org/about/#:~:text=The%20human%2Danimal%20bond%20is,%2C%20animals%2C%20and%20the%20environment.

Wheaton, Oliver. "'Decluttering' after Someone Dies: How and when Should You Do It?" Marie Curie. July 24, 2020. https://www.mariecurie.org.uk/talkabout/articles/decluttering-after-someone-dies/277411.

"When Is It the Right Time for a New Pet?" Lap of Love. Accessed September 24, 2023. https://www.lapoflove.com/blog/pet-loss-support/when-is-the-right-time-for-a-new-pet#:~:text=You%20may%20end%20up%20projecting,about%20your%20previous%20pet%27s%20death.